THE
SECRET
OF GREAT
ENTREPRENEURS

THE
SECRET
OF GREAT
ENTREPRENEURS

How to Become the Most
Powerful Influence for These Times

FRANK LÓPEZ

I celebrate this book because it reveals a hidden secret for many Christian business people, who until now have found it difficult to unite their profession with their desire to serve the Lord. Indeed, they can become a powerful force of influence to establish the Kingdom of God in their nations. Pastor Frank López is the one to teach us about this because he unites his blessed pastoral ministry with a successful business experience that gives him authority on the matter. Do not stop reading this material. You are about to have a secret revealed to you that will make you a 24/7 servant of the Lord!

CARLOS MIRAIDA
Pastor, Iglesia del Centro, Buenos Aires, Argentina
Coordinator, Buenos Aires Pastors Council

I am so happy to read what Pastor Frank wrote on this subject because I know him, and I know with the passion and faith with which he handles these issues. He is a man who loves the Church and understands the level of authority that the church will develop in the end times to break down any opposition that rises against the truth. Frank is wise, focused, very oriented to mentoring people, entrepreneurs or "influencers" of this season. Anyone who has prayed how they can leave a great legacy for their generation should read this book. It's inspiring, insightful, and will educate you on the essentials of being a God-prospered entrepreneur, for the glory of His name. Congratulations, Frank!

—REY MATOS
Senior Pastor, Catacumba 5 Ministry, Puerto Rico

The Secret of the Great Entrepreneurs is a book that will allow entrepreneurs to understand God's purpose of that grace and that "power" granted to "make riches." It is a book that will enable those who dream of being entrepreneurs to align their priorities by asking God first for the "why" before the "how". Pastor Frank is a living testimony of that. *The Secret of Great Entrepreneurs* is a book that everyone should read.

—WILLIAM AND MILAGROS AGUAYO
Pastors, La Casa del Padre
Lima, Peru

Christian entrepreneurs have a great calling and responsibility within God's plan for our times. Their ability and influence are tools God uses in extraordinary ways for His purposes. This is why it is in the heart of God to raise entrepreneurs with more anointing, more resources more influence every day.

Pastor Frank is the wisest and more spiritually understanding person I have ever met; added to his experience in the business field has been vital in his successful task of raising great Christian business leaders. This is a book you don't want to stop reading! In these pages, you will find pure wisdom that will equip you to grow into the relevant entrepreneur God intends to make of you.

—PEDRO F. VILLEGAS
Senior Pastor Life Church
Hollywood, FL, USA

At a time when we are continually being exposed to concepts and models of multiple definitions of what an entrepreneur should be and, above all, a "successful entrepreneur," God raises one of his great ministers in this generation, Pastor Frank López, as an instrument to give us tools us with the wisdom that He has given him towards what it truly is to be an entrepreneur of the Kingdom of God.

To speak of Pastor Frank is to speak a of proven, upright, wise man of God with a great teaching heart, so it is a sure thing that the book you have in your hand will help you to be that entrepreneur that God wants you to be and not who the system wants you to be.

We are at a critical time in which God is raising men and women so, amid the chaos and lack of values that we currently live, they can shine as actual lights of the Lord, in whatever they do from wherever they are. Are you ready for that call? I know you are, because if you have this book at hand, you have understood the importance of what God wants to do with you at this time.

—YESENIA THEN
Founder and Pastor
Ministerio Internacional Soplo de Vida
Dominican Republic

The Secret of Great Entrepreneurs

How to Become the Most Powerful Influence for These Times

© 2022 by Frank Lopez

Translated and edited by: Ofelia Perez

ISBN: 978-1-956625-26-4

e-book ISBN: 978-1-956625-27-1

Printed in the United States of America.

Published by Renacer
www.renaceruno.com

1 2 3 4 5 6 7 8 9 10 11 24 23 22

DEDICATION

I dedicate this book to all the people who have been an influence in my life. My parents, my wife, my children, my pastors, those who were coaches when I played sports in my youth, and so many men and women who, throughout the years, have inspired me to dream. We all need others to be inspired.

I pray that this book can inspire you to dream, to stand up for what is God's, and to conquer new horizons. Above all things, I dedicate this book to the Holy Spirit, who every morning inspires me to believe in and exalt Jesus Christ; and to my wife, Zayda López, who has always been praying, advising, and supporting me. Together we have worked to achieve God's dreams for our lives. Without her, nothing would have been possible.

ACKNOWLEDGEMENTS

I want to thank all the wonderful team God has put in my life. This book has been a work in agreement with so many people who have felt the same call from God to inspire today's entrepreneurs and those that God will be raising.

Thanks to Ángela Suárez, Fabiola Romeo, and Ruth Acevedo for their valuable contribution to making this book.

Thanks to Claudio De Oliveira for your wise advice, hard work, and using your talents to publish books for the glory of God. You are a great entrepreneur of God.

Thanks to Pastor and Evangelist Alberto Mottesi for his influence in my life, his powerful teachings, and the love he always gives my family and me.

Thanks to the Jesus Worship Center Church for the support and the opportunity they give me to disciple them and see them grow in God. It is a great honor for my wife and me to mentor them and challenge them to believe big.

TABLE OF CONTENTS

"I prophesy that a mighty move of the Holy Spirit is coming over women and businessmen. God wants to place his Church in a state of glory, in a position where it has the care and passion of women with wisdom, and a group of men of God with financial power and influence in governments, so they place His Church where it needs to be. Women, get ready because a mighty river is coming over you in Latin America. An army of businessmen rises up; and of women who lend their lives so that God may be present and manifest his glory on planet Earth".

—**FRANK LOPEZ**
Senior Pastor
Jesus Worship Center
Doral, FL, USA

FOREWORD

One of the most important scriptures in the Bible that applies to Christian businessmen is Deuteronomy 8:18: "And you shall remember the LORD your God, for *it is* He who gives you power to get wealth, that He may [a]establish His covenant which He swore to your fathers, as *it is* this day.." Moses related this to the Hebrews shortly before they came into possession of the great wealth in the Promised Land. He said this because the people had just spent hundreds of years in slavery in Egypt. Egypt was a land of great suffering and misery; an economic and social framework driven by the greed and self-centeredness of the Egyptians at the extreme expense of the enslaved Hebrews.

During the next 40 years in the wilderness, God taught his people to trust Him for all their needs, and now they were about to acquire the enormous wealth stored up for them in the land of Canaan.

But all of God's people who entered the Promised Land had never experienced living with wealth of any kind. It was going to be a new experience for all of them and God wanted them to be very aware that He required them to use the new wealth to create a nation inspired by the Kingdom of God. A nation driven by a culture of caring and sharing that Jesus later referred to in Matthew 25 as a sheep nation. A nation of universal prosperity and human flourishing where everyone worshiped the one true God who provided prosperity. Quite the contrary to Egypt.

Dear reader, this has not changed to this day. Our Lord requires that you, the entrepreneurs to whom He has given the power to create wealth, do business with the deliberate intention of establishing His covenant on earth today. His covenant is the creation of the modern sheep nations on earth. If you do this; if you intentionally set out to achieve God's broad national vision with your business, and if you do it His way, He will apply His favor and you will experience His supernatural multiplication. If you do GOD'S WILL, GOD'S WAY, your business, your community, and your nation will prosper.

Before I learned this principle, I was always a $2 million businessman. That was the natural ability that God put into my DNA. In other words, my genetic potential in business maxed out at $2 million.

During the first 22 years I was in business, I had 13 different businesses in 9 different industries in 6 different countries, and no matter how hard I tried, I never got over the $2 million mark in any of those businesses.

Although I was a Christian for 15 of those 22 years. Although I was tithing. Even though I was by far the biggest funder of my church, and I know this because I was on the church board and could see what was coming, that went on for 10 years! But I still never got over what was my natural ability. I never worked in the supernatural and my ground was cursed. God never removed the curse from my soil.

Until one day, when I was completely broke, I learned how to attract God's favor BY DOING GOD'S WILL, GOD'S WAY, and everything changed very quickly. By completely broke I mean I had no money, no assets, and $76,000 in credit card debt. But all of a sudden I skyrocketed FROM DOWN FROM ZERO TO $100 MILLION IN 2 YEARS AND 7 MONTHS.

The reason this happened was because I learned about God's larger vision for the earth, which was to create modern sheep nations as in the Matthew 25 concept of sheep and goat nations. I learned where I fit into this bigger picture in terms of my business and my personal ASSIGNMENT, or why God had put me on earth in the first place. AND, MOST OF ALL, I learned to DO BUSINESS GOD'S WAY. I learned to create wealth without creating poverty. I learned the secrets from Boaz, who became a mighty rich man because he allowed the rest of the community in Bethlehem to reap his success.

As I was doing that, the Lord applied His favor, and He lifted the curse from my soil, and the multiplication was enormous. We are today a nearly two-billion-dollar business by valuation, we have a lot of influence, and we are creating sheep nations all over the world.

Pastor Frank López understands this principle more than any other pastor I have ever met. Pastor Frank has trained his business people so well that more than 100 of them were invited to the White House by the Vice

President of the United States in 2019 to participate in US domestic politics before the election. They went to the White House "so that He establishes the pact that he swore to your parents, as on this day".

I pray that you will use your business to establish God's covenant in your nation and that He will apply His favor so that you collectively create a better world for your people, just as Boaz did in the book of Ruth. God bless you.

—DAVE HODGSON
Managing Director of Paladin Group
Kingdom Founder Investors Ministry
https://www.kingdominvestors.com.au/

INTRODUCTION

We live in a unique moment of powerful influence at high levels through businessmen who are part of the people of God. There is a move of the Holy Spirit to convert God's entrepreneurs into people of high influence in our society. God will put great resources in your hands in all areas: education, health, economics, politics and government, both inside the government and outside.

They will be leaders whose strong influence will affect, not only their generation, but the new generations; leaders with vision, people whose decisions will transcend because they will be heard by those who make decisions for society and nations. God will anoint these entrepreneurs with a vision, they will be received by the highest figures of the countries and they will be able to implement His vision with their influence.

I make it very clear that this move has nothing to do with a prosperity gospel or a love of money that my ministry and I do not preach or enact. It is not about being a rich or prosperous businessman to contribute to the coffers or boast of oneself. This is a move of God for this time (not perpetual), of men and women of God, whose extraordinary prosperity and entrepreneurship will take them to a position where they are called, accepted, listened to and, above all, powerfully influential in the organizations that they decide and implement changes in our society, starting with governments. People who, from their position, will make a call or a contact to be received in terms of present and future negotiations, and will be attended by their power of influence. We know that this interaction already occurs, but not with God's entrepreneurs. This movement has already begun subtly in the Kingdom, but God intends to create a large group of businessmen who represent Him on an international level.

When I talk about entrepreneurs, I emphasize that there is a large movement of women entrepreneurs who will play a leading role within these influential people.

These influential entrepreneurs must have specific attributes:

- Obedience to His Word and the Holy Spirit
- Obedience to pastoral care and authorities.

  a. Because of their work, the enemy is going to attack their families and there will be temptations to resist.
  b. It is necessary to prepare in them a pastoral heart.
  c. There has to be order. God does not give abundance where there is no order.
  d. Accountability is required.

- Know how to channel their influence wisely.
- Obedience to prayer, which is the highest level of honor and worship.
- Have a mentor; a person who opens his life spiritually and from whom the impartation about the Kingdom flows to the disciple. A mentor is much more important than a doctorate in theology . The Biblical pattern of teaching is through mentors; not traditional schools.

The presence and inspiration of the Holy Spirit in this book is to offer you clear and precise mentoring on how to become an influential businessman for God. Chapter by chapter you will read everything you need to become an entrepreneur of God and for God. This Ministry and I are called to be an instrument of this move of the Holy Spirit and it is up to us to equip, prepare and care for these anointed entrepreneurs to be of powerful influence and transform the world.

PART I

THE ENTREPRENEURIAL ANOINTING

"The highest principles of stewardship must stand for the multiplying administration of the goods that God gives us. God adds to those who multiply".

FRANK LOPEZ

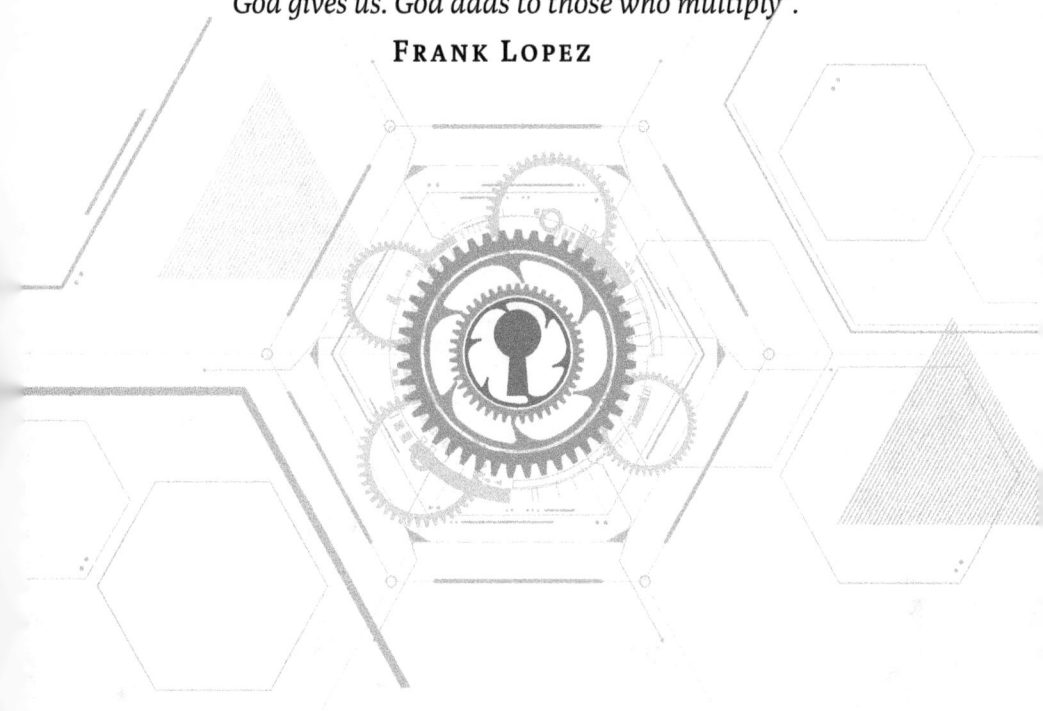

Chapter 1

ENTREPRENEURSHIP

*Her gain and her pay will be set apart for the
LORD; it will not be treasured nor laid up, for
her gain will be for those who dwell before the
LORD, to eat sufficiently, and for fine clothing*

—ISAIAH 23:18

There is a move of the Holy Spirit to raise up men and women with the heart of a servant and the supernatural ability to multiply, in order to take over nations, governments and to be a determining influence in favor of God's purposes. The Church that has no influence, has no power, and the time has already begun for the transfer of power to the hands of the children of God committed to being instruments so that nations and governments live according to the intention that God has always had.

God will put great resources in the hands of these entrepreneurs, in education, and within and outside governments. They will be anointed leaders with a vision, affecting new generations and making decisions on the level of the decision made by Pontius Pilate, which was the most important decision in history.

In order for us to fulfill this lofty purpose, the business vision of the children of God has to be different; it must reflect God's greater vision. If you are a servant of the Lord Jesus, you must see your business as something holy, something pure, like a ministry. You must manage and multiply it with the broad, divine mindset of not only making money for yourself and for the money itself. An important part of wise stewardship is being a living witness to the fulfillment of God's promises when we obey Him, and commit ourselves to being in a position to influence to be an instrument of His plans.

I invite you to read this eloquent parable with different eyes than you have read it before.

The Parable of the Talents

"For *the kingdom of heaven is* like a man traveling to a far country, *who* called his own servants and delivered his goods to them. And to one he gave five talents, to another two, and to another one, to each according to his own ability; and immediately he went on a journey. Then he who had received the five talents went and traded with them, and made another five talents. And likewise he who *had received* two gained two more also. But he who had received one went and dug in the ground, and hid his lord's money. After a long time the lord of those servants came and settled accounts with them. "So he who had received five talents came and brought five other talents, saying, 'Lord, you delivered to me five talents; look, I have gained five more talents besides them.' His lord said to him, 'Well *done,* good and faithful servant; you were faithful over a few things, I will make you ruler over many things. Enter into the joy of your lord.' He also who had received two talents came and said, 'Lord, you delivered to me two talents; look, I have gained two more talents besides them.' His lord said to him, 'Well *done,* good and faithful servant; you have been faithful over a few things, I will make you ruler over many things. Enter into the joy of your lord.' "Then he who had received the one talent came and said, 'Lord, I knew you to be a hard man, reaping where you have not sown, and gathering where you have not scattered seed. And I was afraid, and went and hid your talent in the ground. Look, *there* you have *what is* yours.' "But his lord answered and said to him, 'You wicked and lazy servant, you knew that I reap where I have not sown, and gather where I have not scattered seed. So you ought to have deposited my money with the bankers, and at my coming I would have received back my own with interest. So take the talent from him, and give *it* to him who has ten talents. 'For to everyone who has, more will be given, and he will have abundance; but from him who does not have, even what he has will be taken way. And cast the unprofitable servant into the outer darkness. There will be weeping and gnashing of teeth.'

—MATTHEW 25:14-30

The two key words in this Biblical passage are "servants" and "goods." The servants are:

- Those who belong to their Lord.
- They obey the orders of their Lord.
- They work, they do the work that their Lord needs them to do.
- They are not their own owners.
- His character and his heart are to serve with a spirit of service.
- Nothing belongs to them; everything belongs to their Lord.
- What the Lord gives you has a purpose.

- The Lord expects you to produce, multiply, and be diligent.

Goods, although most people interpret them as something only material, refer to skills; talents; vision; circumstances; opportunities; passion, desire to advance and excel; and divine connections with people who inspire us, teach us and who are open doors.

This is a strong parable that is essential to apply when we talk about God's entrepreneurs. Here Jesus speaks with all authority and demonstrates the consequences if one does not work diligently and courageously. Diligence, work and bravery will be rewarded with more than we produce. But the lack of diligence, fear, ignoring and valuing the goods, will be rewarded with less, or will not be compensated. Everything that God gives us is to multiply it.

God calls "servants" those who are His extension on earth; that his hands, his feet, and his mouth are here to do His works. When we only think of ourselves, that is selfishness. Seeking our personal interest based on the self, the ego, disqualifies us from being His servants and that has horrible consequences such as fear and doubt in what you do, especially in what you undertake.

When your gaze is on you, you will have fear. When your eyes are on Jesus, nothing will stop you.

A company in the hands of His servants is a ministry, because you are His servant. And if you are His servant, you are anointed by Him to produce more, multiply and wisely manage God's goods in your life. You must always have a servant heart for God to prosper you.

....

When your gaze is on you, you will
have fear. When your eyes are on
Jesus, nothing will stop you.

....

You can prosper with your tricks, killing yourself, working, but everything you produce without God will curse you. Everything will control you, because there are demonic agents assigned to riches. Never sell yourself, or be dazzled by how much money they offer you, if it is not what God is giving you. In the business world Satan deceives us. Be careful not to fall into their traps; make sure you are a faithful servant of the Lord always.

The Word says:

The blessing of the LORD makes *one* rich, and He adds no sorrow with it.

—PROVERBS 10:22

God gives the goods to His servants because He loves them and blesses them. In this parable, which speaks specifically about money and business, He distributed the talents according to the abilities, but this action was really a test because God will always test you before giving you the dream that He has for you. Before the servants began God's dream, God's mission, He called them to account for those talents He had given them.

When God asked them to account for the talents, those who multiplied the talents were praised by Him, saying to them: "Good faithful servant, you have been faithful over a little, I will put you over much¨. Much of God brings joy. But when the third servant, to whom he gave a talent, had hidden it, he took it from him and said: " You wicked and lazy servant..." And after taking away his talent, he cast him out into the darkness, so that there would be crying and gnashing of teeth. Said servant embraced fear.

As an entrepreneur never be afraid because that paralyzes God's plans for you. God demands profit and fruit from you. Investing where it is not produced does not serve God nor does it serve you. Invest where fruit is produced, where there is transformation. God gave that hidden talent to the one who had ten talents, because His Word says *that* "'For to everyone who has, more will be given, and he will have abundance; but from him who does not have, even what he has will be taken way". The multiplication of God is His glory. When God says that he who has will be given more, he is referring to the one who has:

- **Vision** to multiply
- **Faith** to believe
- **Diligence** to work

....

Never be afraid because that paralyzes God's plans for you.

....

Prayer is the prelude to doing and wanting. However, in addition to praying and fasting, it takes diligence, vision, and faith to multiply God's resources. God's company is the most complicated, but the most blessed when you become his servant and obey him in everything.

A servant is one who obeys the commands of his Lord. When you are a prosperous servant, you must not make the mistake of dividing or sowing where you want. You must first ask God: What do you want me to do with the goods you have given me? Do not sow unless God commands you to sow. Beware of the pride of pretending to be good, helping many people to look at you. That is a sin; that is not being a servant.

If you think about it, you shouldn't even need to ask God where to sow, because you are supposed to be connected to God's heart at all times, and as servants we belong to Him. Identity and value are given to you by the King of Kings, Lord of Lords. Do not take examples from the world, because you are not of the world. Do not attend traditional conventions of the world that only feed the ego and the flesh. None of that gives you the true identity.

We work because God needs us to work and produce. What matters is that you put yourself in the call, in the assignment of God; in the river of God that prospers. That's when the heavens open up to you, and there is no devil or anything that can stop you. A servant does what the Lord needs him to do. Your character and your heart must be to serve him. We are not servants of money, of greed. We must not operate in the self. We must operate in Him. That does not mean that you do not prosper and that you do not have many assets. It means that you prosper connected to Him, guided by Him, obedient to the call of God in you. There is no greater privilege than knowing and serving the Lord of Lords. Nothing blesses more than exercising the stewardship of his goods as He has assigned us.

God is going to test us to give us the entrepreneurial anointing with the purpose of transforming entire nations. Receiving this anointing demands administering what God gives us with holiness, diligence and submission to his will, obeying him in everything. If you are a businessman and you are stealing tithes, do not expect God to prosper you.

When you honor God, He will set you before kings. When we only think about ourselves, we lose, we are disqualified. We must think first of Him and that we are His servants.

....

If you are a businessman and you are stealing tithes, do not expect God to prosper you.

....

We are going to work on what He wants us to work on. Let's not accept fear and let's manage what God gives us, without fear. Let's not ignore God's commands. God does not want anyone to be lost.

Chapter 2

GOD GIVES THE POWER TO MAKE RICHES

*And you shall remember the LORD your God,
for it is He who gives you power to get wealth,
that He may [a]establish His covenant which
He swore to your fathers, as it is this day.*

—DEUTERONOMY 8:18

For many years, thousands of people have thought that being poor is a virtue or a lifestyle that brings them closer to God. There is nothing further from reality. Our connection with God is not established by sacrifices of poverty or scarcity. On the contrary, God wants us to live abundantly and to acquire wealth to help those in need and to establish His kingdom on earth.

The sacrifice of Jesus made us completely free. It was necessary to cut off Satan's bondage and oppression over our lives. For these reasons and many others, we can be sure that God's will for us is that we have life in abundance. This is how he expresses it in his Word.

> And you shall remember the LORD your God, for *it is* He who gives you power to get wealth, that He may establish His covenant which He swore to your fathers, as *it is* this day.
>
> —JOHN 10:10

That life in abundance encompasses all our areas; including health, family and finances.

The good use of economic resources gives us the possibility of fulfilling on a large scale the Great Commission of taking the message of love to all people. The Ggospel and the message of salvation have reached the most remote corners of the world thanks to the economic power of those who have financed evangelization in great crusades, missionary programs and through the media.

In the Bible we can see that, from the beginning, God has established that it is He who gives us power to successfully undertake, develop and establish whatever we are willing to do. In this book we will talk about the power to get rich and how God empowers his people in order to fulfill the Great Commission that all know him.

God is first. Everything begins with Him because it is He who begins everything as the great Creator. God desires that your relationship with Him never changes, and that your reverence and honor of Him as God never be affected. He wants to continue to be heard by you and expects obedience from you. The Church is the bride of Jesus and this must be your absolute priority.

God gives the power. He is the one who anoints someone with a specific purpose, and gives each person different gifts and talents that we see reflected as something innate in each one. In the same way, it guides us in undertakings where we need supernatural power to fulfill the mission, and gives us the power to make riches. That power is not given to everyone, but everyone has access to that power.

We can always surrender and cry out to God for his anointing and power in business, to generate economic performance that allows us to achieve our goals at any level because we have access to the power that God gives us when we connect with Him.

God is a God of covenants. Every covenant that He makes, He keeps, because God is faithful. In a pact there are specific agreements by both parties; we must always do our part in obedience.

....

*According to your heart, according to your
obedience and according to how you honor God,
you will receive what you are waiting for.*

....

EVERYTHING BELONGS TO GOD

We are simply stewards or administrators of the riches that God places in our hands. Nothing belongs to us forever. However, in this life we must make good use of all the goods that God gives us.

The silver *is* Mine, and the gold *is* Mine,' says the LORD of hosts. 'The glory of this latter temple shall be greater than the former,' says the LORD of hosts. 'And in this place I will give peace,' says the LORD of hosts.
—HAGGAI 2:8-9

God is the owner of all the prosperity that we can have on this earth. When He intervenes, great changes occur. His intervention reverses scarcity, changes our destiny and makes everything rise to a higher level. If before we made riches in the way of the world, what we do with God will be much more excellent. If before we worked tirelessly to achieve riches, now they will flow so that we can have time with our family. God transforms everything in his path. When He intervenes in our lives and in our company, everything changes for the better.

BIBLICAL PROSPERITY IS A GIFT FROM GOD

O LORD, how manifold are Your works! In wisdom
You have made them all.
The earth is full of Your possessions—

— PSALM 104:24

God has created everything on earth for us. The earth is full of blessings, as well as our daily lives.

As for every man to whom God has given riches and wealth, and given him power to eat of it, to receive his [a]heritage and rejoice in his labor—this *is* the gift of God.

—ECCLESIASTES 5:19

God is good. In His grace and mercy, He is willing to prosper us; for His kindness and for honoring what He sees in us.

THE POWER OF GOD HAS A PURPOSE

Riches have the capacity to become your God, if you give them a very big place in your heart. It is one thing to yearn for wealth and financial abundance with the purpose of progressing, blessing your family and doing good in general, positively affecting your environment collectively. Another thing is ambition. If you focus your attention on riches, you would be taking the most important place away from God and our God is a jealous God.

The power of God to make riches is not a reward for your service, or for your devotion, but it comes through your obedience and the surrender of your heart, which learns to put God first. Putting God first means putting His will above all things. In the new covenant of grace and salvation through faith in Christ Jesus, His will is to save, heal, restore, and cover entire nations with His truth. His presence and attention, His ability and His anointing have specific purposes, goals that He wants to accomplish. Everything has to do with the redemption of the human being; God's covenant.

In the case of Abraham, called the Father of Faith, God made covenants that affected many generations, including land to form a nation, resources to finance their establishment, and His support when they stayed in the covenant. As with the children of Abraham, God supports the work of our hands with His divine favor, His divine protection, and His constant blessing.

This covenant was kept for entire generations and at that time, people recognized the power that God gave to some to make riches. Let's see how this was reflected in Isaac's life:

> Then Isaac sowed in that land, and reaped in the same year a hundredfold; and the LORD blessed him. The man began to prosper, and continued prospering until he became very prosperous; for he had possessions of flocks and possessions of herds and a

great number of servants. So the Philistines envied him. Now the Philistines had stopped up all the wells which his father's servants had dug in the days of Abraham his father, and they had filled them with earth. And Abimelech said to Isaac, "Go away from us, for you are much mightier than we".

—GENESIS 26:12-16

The Bible states that He is the one who gives us **power** to **make** riches. In another version, it tells us that He is the one who gives us the **strength** to get rich. Whether you call it power, strength, or favor of God, riches are made, they are obtained, they do not fall from heaven, but it is Biblical that God gives us the strategies. Let us think that God gives you a seed, but you must prepare the land, water it and take care of it to obtain the plant and, consequently, its fruit.

That is our part: the diligence, work, love and faith that we put into doing everything with excellence. God never blesses laziness or mediocrity, much less lack of responsibility. The concept of faith that promotes being still and not working is a wrong way of believing.

There is a capacity that He wants to deposit in someone in order for His covenant to be established. The book of Galatians, in the New Testament, refers to this covenant made by God with Abraham:

Just as Abraham "believed God, and it was accounted to him for righteousness." Therefore know that *only* those who are of faith are sons of Abraham. And the Scripture, foreseeing that God would justify the Gentiles by faith, preached the gospel to Abraham beforehand, *saying,* "In you all the nations shall be blessed." So then those who *are* of faith are blessed with believing Abraham (Galatians 3:6-9).

That the blessing of Abraham might come upon the Gentiles in Christ Jesus, that we might receive the promise of the Spirit through faith.

— GALATIANS 3:14

This blessing of abundance is not only for the Hebrew people. In Christ Jesus is also for the Gentiles.

Chapter 3

BUSINESS IN HIS PERFECT WILL

That the blessing of Abraham might come
upon the Gentiles in Christ Jesus, that we might
receive the promise of the Spirit through faith.

—PSALM 143:10

There are many important aspects to growing a business. One of them is the knowledge of the market, because through the study of consumers and their needs, as well as the competition, the best marketing strategies can be designed. In this regard, seeking expert advice is very wise. The selection of personnel and specialists in each area of our service cannot be ignored either.

But above all natural aspects, we need to align our lives in the perfect will of God. We talk about God's order in our lives, putting our relationship with Him first, then our family, our ministry, and then our work. This order lies in the heart. It may be that we spend more time at work than at home, or that the times of intimacy with God have a short duration with respect to the time we spend working. However, God must be in our hearts at all times and when choosing, making big decisions, the family must be our main focus.

The human being very easily forgets the origin of his well-being. We need, first of all, to learn about the things that God does and his purposes. God is a God of deals and covenants. For example: marriage is a covenant. Salvation is a covenant. God made a covennt with his son Jesus Christ and told him: Everyone who believes in your sacrifice, everyone who honors your blood, I honor him with eternal life.

....

God is a God of deals and covenants.

....

In a covenant between two people, there are conditions and instructions that both parties must comply with. In this case we will apply it to how to get rich in financial terms, understanding that the verse from Deuteronomy 8:18 quoted in the previous chapter can be applied to all areas of life, since God's protection and the power we have in Him is fully reflected when we live in Him. When we learn to receive the power or strength to multiply, we see the results because God multiplies what we have. I remind you that this power is available to everyone, but only those who learn it can receive it.

Deuteronomy 8:18 tells us about our fallen nature. Human beings are selfish and seek what suits us. That is why we easily forget about God and his blessings. We learn to remember what God has done and is doing for us. No one is born with the ability to do so. In bad times or good times, we have to put God first.

God wants us to love Him because he first loved us, but His infinite love wants to have our hearts to keep Him safe and to bless us. When God is in the first place in your life, then you receive power and strength to obtain riches.

The supremacy of God is so important that we must reinforce this teaching on essential points in these mentioned verses.

1. God is first. It all starts with Him. He wants to continue to be heard by you. And expect obedience.
2. God wants you to obey so your heart doesn't go astray.

3. God gives the power to get riches. He has the ability to anoint someone for a specific purpose.

4. God is a covenant God. The covenant that He makes, He fulfills and there are specific agreements by both parties.

5. God does not give to everyone the ability to get rich, but everyone has access to that power.

6. According to your heart, according to your obedience and according to how you honor God, wealth has the ability to become your god. And our God is a jealous God.

7. This power to make wealth is not a reward for your service, or for your devotion. It comes through your obedience to God and your heart, which learns to put God first.

8. Putting God first means putting His will above all things in the new covenant of grace and salvation through faith in Christ Jesus.

....

His will is to save, heal, restore and cover entire nations with His truth.

....

INTIMACY WITH GOD IS ESSENTIAL

An indisputable part of putting God first is having a life of intimacy with God. Thus, we will hear the sighs of His heart. The way we are intimate with God is simple: we just need to invite Him and He comes.

Then, to establish that intimate bond that allows us to know the heart of God, listen to His voice and have His guidance, we must:

- First, accept the invitation that God makes us.
- Connect more deeply with God.
- Being close to Him, listening to His heart.
- Be sensitive to your voice.
- Seek Him constantly.
- Intimacy with God is something that we must look for in the reading of the Bible, in a church where Jesus Christ is preached as the only Savior and in our times of prayer.

Start each day seeking intimacy with God, inviting Him to live with you each day, involving Him in everything: your home, your business, your decisions, your family. See to it that He remains in everything. When you involve God in your life first, you will get to know Him better each day and as you obey Him, He will reward that obedience.

While you are in intimacy with God, you should tell Him: "Watch my mouth, watch my decisions, watch my heart, guide me, Lord, prevent me from making mistakes and if I'm doing it wrong, stop that project or action". This is called causing intimacy with God. The instructions for our life and our success are in privacy.

The instructions you need for your business are in intimacy with God. When you bring God into your business, you bring multiplication into your business. Intimacy is in prayer.

Ask God to tell you exactly what He wants you to do, because God is a God of assignments. Your business must be a divine assignment from heaven; and the assignment He gives, He backs up. For that reason, you should ask God about the people, the moments, the places and everything that surrounds an important project, so that He can guide you along the way.

....

The instructions you need for your business are in intimacy with God. When you bring God into your business, you bring multiplication into your business. Intimacy is in prayer.

....

God helps you in everything because He loves you, but His support is different. We must seek His full support, which occurs when we walk in His will for us. Ask God specifically to show you what your assignment is. If God asked you not to get involved in a business, no matter how good you look at it, don't get involved. Do not be guided by the numbers; Guide yourself by the voice of your Lord that multiplies the numbers. As a consequence of this order in our lives, of the priority we give to God, of our intimacy with Him, we will be more sensitive to the Holy Spirit, we will be able to listen to His requests and by obeying Him, we will have a reward.

Read this example:

Then as he talked with them, there was the champion, the Philistine of Gath, Goliath by name, coming up from the armies of the Philistines; and he spoke according to the same words. So David heard *them*. And all the men of Israel, when they saw the man, fled from him and were dreadfully afraid. So the men of Israel said, "Have you seen this man who has come up? Surely he has come up to defy Israel; and it shall be *that* the man who kills him the king will enrich with great riches, will give him his daughter, and give his father's house exemption *from taxes* in Israel." Then David spoke to the men who stood by him, saying, "What shall be done for the man who kills this Philistine and takes away the reproach from Israel? For who *is* this uncircumcised Philistine, that he should defy the armies of the living God?".

—1 SAMUEL 17: 23-26)

In this passage King Saul offered great reward to whoever faced the giant.

It consisted of a lot of money, his daughter in marriage, and no more taxes for the rest of his life.

If we look at the biblical context, David's family business consisted of raising sheep and trading their produce. In modern times we could say that he was the *manager* or manager of this company. Being a shepherd of sheep, he was assigned to bring assistance to his brothers. But this assignment was changed by God on the way, for a task that ended in facing the giant victoriously. As a reward for that obedience to God, David received what King Saul had offered.

In the face of great threats to his people, God will ask his anointed for great deeds and will reward them greatly.

We have to be attentive to God's instructions, we have to obey and we will make great profits. David's vision was to uphold the name of God, the reputation of his God, and the power of the covenant that God had made with Israel. God's vision was to reward obedience. David didn't know what was going on, he didn't know about the reward. But he was attentive to the voice of God and to obey him immediately. David had to react to what he was seeing for the first time. David allowed himself to be carried away by the impulse of the Holy Spirit and the zeal that God had placed in his heart for his people. David obeyed God and received his reward.

· ·

In the face of great threats to his people, God will ask his anointed for great deeds and will reward them greatly.

· ·

Fear always gets in the way. But David was not afraid and faced the giant. And as a result of that intimacy with God, he listened to what he had to do and he overcame. From the human point of view, it was a business transaction between King Saul and David. But it really was an assignment from God to His anointed and God rewarded David.

Do not be afraid to react to things that God asks of you, that you have not done before, because God's reward is in obedience and in the faith that He will not leave you alone in your process. In the process of obeying him, you may have to go against human logic. Even on those occasions, trust, because there is no such thing as failure in God. It doesn't matter what others say or think; that you care about God's instructions above all opinions. Obedience is an act of faith. Obedience activates the multiplication of heaven.

All entrepreneurs have a specific assignment, and every day we have to invite God into our lives, to find direction to execute it. God's assignments grow and change like a seed to what God wants us to do. He gives us the instructions that require obedience.

God's vision and instructions do not usually happen by themselves; they need human participation. God does everything, but you have to say yes. That is called obedience. Obedience is something that God seeks; He does it with a purpose. Obedience always comes before reward. This is a sign of a true relationship with God; a sign that there is oil in your lamp. Obedience becomes a sign that we are under a covenant with Him.

....

All entrepreneurs have a specific assignment.

....

God does not want a relationship with you to use you, but to love you. Likewise, we should want a relationship with God to love him, not to use Him. He who

loves unites, seeks harmony. Seeking God and his blessings for the sole purpose of making money is like using
it as an amulet; it is sin, it is shameful. God knows the
heart inside; we cannot deceive Him. We must seek God
to love, serve and honor Him. When we do and delight
in Him, He grants the desires of our hearts.

> Delight yourself also in the Lord, and He shall give
> you the desires of your heart.
>
> (PSALMS 37:4)

God will purposefully ask you for obedience. It will
give you instructions to see what you do. He tests us to
make sure we are prepared for the assignment, the divine purpose. We have to understand that we are on a
constant assignment and that assignment always has to
do with God's justice.

God speaks things to you in private, that at the moment you do not understand. But when the devil rises up
against you, you understand and remember what God has
told you in private. By this I mean that when you main-
tain an intimate communication with God, He will even
warn you of the attacks that will be raised against you.
When you disobey, you give the enemy license to destroy
your plans; for that reason, you must stay aligned to the
will of God. He will give us strategies in advance to know
how to act in each battle. This is how David, when he
heard the voice of the giant, remembered what God had
said to him, and he obeyed God and received his reward.

....

*God always wins, no matter
how big your enemy is.*

....

SUCCESS IS IN OBEYING

In David's case, the success was that he was always attentive to God's instructions. Thus, we must be attentive to God's instructions and to the changes of assignment that He may give us along the way.

Just as God told Abraham to establish the culture of obeying God so that generations would not forget the promises that God had given him, the calling of your children and grandchildren begins with you. God is a God of generations.

We have to build businesses with a generational vision, involving our children. United families make businesses.

David's reward came in addition. Our vision must not seek personal gain. God knew David's heart and the zeal that boy felt for God's people. David sought to vindicate the army of Israel, which was terrified of this giant. His motivation was not personal glory; however, it came to him. His vision was not in the reward, but in what God had spoken to him.

....

*We have to build businesses with a
generational vision, involving our children.
United families make businesses.*

....

If you put your business in God's hands and have God's zeal to defend His Word and establish His kingdom on earth, you will defend His name, you will put it on high and you will see how God will multiply your business. God is going to add personal gain to you better than you can imagine.

> Now therefore, if you will indeed obey My voice and keep My covenant, then you shall be a special treasure to Me above all people; for all the earth *is* Mine.
> —EXODUS 19:5

Here the Bible reaffirms to us that if we listen to God's voice and keep His covenant, we will be His special treasure and He will reward us if we obey Him.

God is the one who has given you the gifts you have and the opportunities that have brought you here. You were created and placed by God in this time, to bring the heavens to earth, so that your business prospers, to give employment to families, so that the truth of Christ is established in the nations. You are a special treasure of Almighty God. That's you.

The next verse in this portion of the book of Exodus says:

> And you shall be to Me a kingdom of priests and a holy nation. These *are* the words which you shall speak to the children of Israel.
> —EXODUS 19:6

This scripture also tells us that we will be a kingdom of priests; a priest is one who intercedes. Your identity as an entrepreneur involves being an intercessor of God. As a consequence, we must take the government to intercede as an army of God's businessmen to solve the problems, to straighten what is crooked.

If we look at it from a business perspective, what happened in that passage was God's business transaction, not David's. David acted according to his zeal for God and heeded the instructions that God had given him in private, as well as the prompting of the Holy Spirit within him. David's friendship with God transcends throughout his life. Even in the moments when David failed and sinned, he always returned to seek his intimacy with God, because it was true.

> You are My friends if you do whatever I command you. No longer do I call you servants, for a servant does not know what his master is doing; but I have called you friends, for all things that I heard from My Father I have made known to you.
>
> —JOHN 15:14-15

This beautiful passage explains the wonderful connection that Jesus made with his disciples. They were His friends, they had been with Him, traveling, working, carrying out His ministry, the divine assignment that the heavenly Father had given Him; they were His team. He called them friends.

We, as followers of Jesus, are His team. We are His hands and feet in the Land of the Living. We have the assignment to follow His instructions embodied in the Bible and the instructions that the Holy Spirit, the Comforter that He left us, gives us in every situation. God makes known to us everything we need to know about how to take the business to other levels according to His will, as long as we seek Him, listen to Him in private and obey Him in everything.

In this wonderful friendship, God shares with us His zeal, His desires and His plans. That is what makes you a radical intercessor. To radical intercessors, God opens the heavens. Relationship and intimacy are a formula that leads us to follow instructions. Get used to seeking God's instructions first, to make decisions in your business.

Chapter 4

THE GOSPEL OF JESUS CHRIST: TRANSFORMATION AND MULTIPLICATION

For I am not ashamed of the gospel [a]of Christ, for it is the power of God to salvation for everyone who believes, for the Jew first and also for the Greek. For in it the righteousness of God is revealed from faith to faith; as it is written, "The just shall live by faith." For the wrath of God is revealed from heaven against all ungodliness and unrighteousness of men, who suppress the truth in unrighteousness, because what may be known of God is manifest in them, for God has shown it to them.

—ROMANS 1:16-19

The Gospel is God's transforming power to take the ordinary and make it extraordinary. It is the power of God for salvation, eternal life, healing and prosperity. The Gospel of Jesus Christ is not just a message of hope, healing, and redemption. All of that is part of the Gospel, but God's intention is to transform.

By his Word everything has been done:

- He spoke and there was light.
- He spoke, and chaos and disorder ceased to be.
- He spoke and healed. His Word makes sickness flee.
- He spoke, and removed the lamentation and despair.

THE MIRACULOUS CATCH AND BUSINESS

There are many ups and downs in business life. A business can boom and bust, or it can become an ordeal just starting a business. Sometimes, God allows the entrepreneur to make all the decisions that he thinks are right, and yet there comes a time when the lack of results leads him to cry out for a new strategy.

It is then that God gives a Word, an order, a vision.

If the person listens and obeys, we can see great miracles happen, just like at the beginning of time.

The Bible speaks of a miraculous catch, where skilled men in the trade of fishing throughout their lives had thrown the nets with the experience they had, and nothing happened. Let's see how divine intervention and obedience of those men changed everything.

....

If the person listens and obeys, we can see great miracles happen, just like at the beginning of time.

....

So it was, as the multitude pressed about Him to hear the word of God, that He stood by the Lake of Gennesaret, and saw two boats standing by the lake; but the fishermen had gone from them and were washing *their* nets. Then He got into one of the boats, which was Simon's, and asked him to put out a little from the land. And He sat down and taught the multitudes from the boat. When He had stopped speaking, He said to Simon, "Launch out into the deep and let down your nets for a catch." But Simon answered and said to Him, "Master, we have toiled all night and caught nothing; nevertheless at Your word I will let down the net." And when they had done this, they caught a great number of fish, and their net was breaking. So they signaled to *their* partners in the other boat to come and help them. And they came and filled both the boats, so that they began to sink. When Simon Peter saw *it,* he fell down at Jesus' knees, saying, "Depart from me, for I am a sinful man, O Lord!" For he and all who were with him were astonished at the catch of fish which they had taken; and so also *were* James and John, the sons of Zebedee, who were partners with Simon. And Jesus said to Simon, "Do not be afraid. From now on you will catch men."

—LUKE 5:1-10

If you study the passage well, you see that God sends His Word to man, man receives it and activates it through obedience, and then miracles happen.

For Peter, this was an example of how the *Rhema* of God (a timely word of God inspired by the Holy Spirit, which brings life, power and faith to realize and fulfill it) and the obedience of a man, when united, bring multiplication, abundance and economic miracles. Peter did not set his sights only on the profit that would come into his pocket, but on the great discovery of the power of God in front of him. The miraculous catch means: I, Jesus Christ, get into your business, I will give you information and instructions; and then you will see miracles. In conclusion, in this passage of the miraculous catch...

....

God sends His Word to man, man receives it and activates it through obedience, and then miracles happen.

....

1. Jesus fills everything. He takes the void and makes it overflow as He did with the two boats.
2. Peter passed the test. He could see the glory of God in abundance.

3. The first thing Peter did was honor Jesus; abundance did not take the first place away from Jesus.
4. Peter obeyed and saw the Glory of God in abundance.

In the Gospel message we find that applying God's wisdom and principles produces great results. The Gospel of Jesus Christ has the power to transform scarcity into abundance, to make the land fertile, and to cause God to bless your hands and cause your sowing to be multiplied far beyond one hundred percent.

The constant reading of the Bible is a training to achieve a life full of wonderful fruits. Among many things, we find the secrets and the power to get rich, we learn how to work with what we have and we learn to improve ourselves, to work and to multiply.

> Blessed *is* the man who walks not in the counsel of
> the ungodly, nor stands in the path of sinners, nor
> sits in the seat of the scornful; But his delight *is* in
> the law of the Lord, and in His law he [b]meditates
> day and night. He shall be like a tree
> Planted by the [c]rivers of water, that brings forth its
> fruit in its season, whose leaf also shall not wither;
> and whatever he does shall prosper.
>
> —Psalm 1:1-3

....

God is the God of multiplication. With God
you can prosper. with God you will prosper!

....

Delighting in obeying God and meditating on His
Word makes us prosper spiritually and also in this natural world, because we become recipients of God's power.

PART II

THE POWER OF OBEDIENCE

"God's plan is great. And always much bigger than yours. For God's plan to be established on your plan, it takes obedience. Obedience is the door to the prosperity that God has prepared for His children".

—FRANK LOPEZ

Chapter 5

GOD OF ORDER AND STRUCTURE

*A wicked man hardens his face, but as for
the upright, he [a]establishes his way.*

—Proverbs 21:29

We need to establish God's righteousness in our lives so that we can be counted as righteous in the midst of the world in which we live. We also know that obedience is the key to blessing and multiplication. How do we start?

The first thing is to establish order. God is a God of order. Where there is no order, the Lord waits until there is order to visit you. The devil visits disorder. If you are not in order, you are inviting the devil to visit your company, your home, your ministry, your finances. Everything has to be in order so that the devil does not visit you because the devil visits the disorder of Christians.

God's order has to do with our priorities. We must keep in mind that God wants us to give priority to Him; soon after comes our family. This is not because God wants to be the center of our attention as a self-centered requirement, but because it is the way we can receive His attributes and stay connected to His power to overcome difficulties and walk in His divine plan.

Next after God, the priority is our family. We should not postpone our time with the family for the time we dedicate to our company or business. Let us understand, of course, that in every beginning it is necessary to make sacrifices and we will not always be at home. However, there are times and circumstances when we must choose to be with family. In this sense, even if it is not a lot of time a day, let it be quality time.

God is a God of structure. He makes structures of men to manifest His peace, His blessing, His protection; structures of men that feed, advise, guide and minister.

When the Spirit of God meets that structure in the Biblical order, He flows there. Where there is no order, there is no Holy Spirit. The Holy Spirit does not visit where there are no structures of men.

You can operate in the gifts of the Holy Spirit without the Holy Spirit, because God gives gifts and takes them away. One day He will ask you to account for those gifts: if you used them under His cover or if you used them on your flesh under the anointing of the devil, because the devil also anoints. But when the Holy Spirit finds a structure in order according to the Bible, to the advice of the Word of God, there flows teaching, advice, guidance, the power of glory and blessing. There are living waters where He plants you and your leaf does not fall. There everything you do prospers. He takes care of you, of wolves, deceit and even of emotions that can confuse you. The Holy Spirit looks for human structures in order to flow.

> And so it was, on the next day, that Moses sat to judge the people; and the people stood before Moses from morning until evening. So when Moses' father-in-law saw all that he did for the people, he said, "What *is* this thing that you are doing for the people? Why do you alone [a]sit, and all the people stand before you from morning until evening?" And Moses said to his father-in-law, "Because the people come to me to inquire of God. When they have a [b]difficulty, they come to me, and I judge between one and another; and I make known the statutes of God and His laws."

So Moses' father-in-law said to him, "The thing that you do *is* not good. Both you and these people who *are* with you will surely wear yourselves out. For this thing *is* too much for you; you are not able to perform it by yourself. Listen now to my voice; I will give you [c]counsel, and God will be with you: Stand before God for the people, so that you may bring the difficulties to God. And you shall teach them the statutes and the laws, and show them the way in which they must walk and the work they must do. Moreover you shall select from all the people able men, such as fear God, men of truth, hating covetousness; and place *such* over them *to be* rulers of thousands, rulers of hundreds, rulers of fifties, and rulers of tens. And let them judge the people at all times. Then it will be *that* every great matter they shall bring to you, but every small matter they themselves shall judge. So it will be easier for you, for they will bear *the burden* with you. If you do this thing, and God *so* commands you, then you will be able to endure, and all this people will also go to their place in peace." So Moses heeded the voice of his father-in-law and did all that he had said. And Moses chose able men out of all Israel, and made them heads over the people: rulers of thousands, rulers of hundreds, rulers of fifties, and rulers of tens. So they judged the people at all times; the hard[d] cases they brought to Moses, but they judged every small case themselves.

—EXODUS 18:13-26

In the book of Exodus, Moses spent 40 years preparing for His call. The call of Moses was multiple. He was the leader, the liberator of Israel. Israel had been 400 years in the world of sin, in slavery. Egypt means "slaves of sin". And the Lord raised up a leader named Moses. Before being a great leader. he herded his father-in-law's sheep.

Moses had a lot of backing from God. God spoke to him face to face and he obeyed God's advice. That's why they said he was a meek man. A meek man is a person who listens to the advice of God, who values the advice of God and does the advice of God. Obeying God's counsel gives you a lot of authority, giving you backing. God plants you in streams of water and everything you do prospers.

Everything that Moses did prosper, but the time came when he could no longer handle the people. Seeing this, his father-in-law asked him why he was doing all the work alone, because if he continued like this he would faint, because it was too much. He told him that was not right. Here we wonder why if Moses spoke face to face with God, God did not tell Him directly; he had to tell his father-in-law.

We see how God uses human authority structures to guide you. In the spiritual world His father-in-law was His father, as are your in-laws in the spiritual world; people of authority in the natural and in the spiritual at the same time. His father-in-law, a noble man, gave advice to a leader of an entire nation of millions. His leadership was spiritual, administrative, governmental.

The first government leader of Israel was Moses. The nation of Israel settled in the desert before reaching the promised land. They already came as a nation and established themselves as such, when God gave Moses the moral code of a nation, the Tablets of the Law. When his father-in-law spoke to him, he told him to listen to Him and God would be with Him. He told him: you are for the people before God and you submit matters to God and teach them the ordinances, the laws. Show them the ways they should walk and what they should do. You choose, from among all the people, men of virtue, men who fear God, men of truth who hate avarice and set them over the people as leaders of thousands, of hundreds and of fifties and of ten.

Look at the detail of the order, the formation of the teams and the orders that you should give them, so that they really help you. They would judge the people at all times and bring all serious matters to him. They would judge everything small, thus lightening the load on him and carrying it with them. If he did this and God commanded him, he would be able to sustain himself and all the people could go in peace to the place where they should go.

See how the human structure of authority and word order bring peace to the people. Peace is the word "shalom", which speaks of prosperity, finding answers, moving forward, walking, not being stagnant; talk about solutions. That which robs you of peace, God can eliminate it. "Shalom" speaks of healing, restoration, peace. And Moses heard the voice of his father-in-law. Moses' leadership was not just because God spoke to him directly. Moses' leadership was also because God spoke to him through others. It gave him a structure of order to shepherd the people.

Operating on Biblical foundations is part of the order. In the Bible we find clear instructions for life and answers to every question. It is necessary that every time we are going to make a decision, we pray and ask for God's direction. One of the ways that He speaks to us is through His Word. Something that goes against the Word of God will not prosper in the lives of those whom God wants to be able to be part of His army, establishing His Kingdom on Earth.

Excellence and obedience are essential attitudes for prosperity in the order and structure of God. Let's look at them in detail in the following chapters.

Chapter 6

ATTITUDE OF EXCELLENCE

Blessed are the undefiled in the way,
who walk in the law of the Lord!

—Psalm 119:1

We see the attitude of excellence in creation, in redemption and in its provision. We must have first excellence for God, family and work. All dealings in our lives are designed to develop in us the spirit of excellence.
Let's define the word excellence:

- Top quality
- Atribute that establishes recognition
- The extra that cancels out the ordinary
- Kindness that attracts special attention
- I treat others with respect, courtesy, appreciation, importance and dignity
- A genuine intention to appreciate, value and give the best
- Being grateful and caring, valuing, adding, contributing so that something is better; level of priority that we express.

What is spirit of excellence?

- It is an attitude that becomes part of your way of life, it is a lifestyle.
- In your spirit you value the revelation that God is present in everything that you are present.
- You give the best of yourself; you persevere and seek to improve yourself more and more.
- An attitude of not settling for enough, but dreaming and activating your dream to overcome what you have achieved. That gives us vision and motivation to work.

God cares about excellence. Everything He does reflects His passion for excellence. He looks at the way we do things. You care about quality. He works hard and cares that things go well. It is checked if there is consideration, efficiency, justice and correct attitudes.

Our God is God of excellence! His dealings in our lives are designed to develop in us a superior attitude and that we learn to give and do our best. Mediocrity, conformism, not wanting to learn more, criticism, contempt, gossip are enemies of excellence. It is a demonic spirit of poverty, of misery that sets identity and establishes generational curses. Mediocrity destroys or cancels excellence; therefore, it is opposite to God.

When you put the greatest interest and give the best of yourself, that defines an attitude of excellence. Excellence is a principle of honor, respect, and love of life; its consequence is always prosperity.

> And whatever you do, do it heartily, as to the Lord and not to men, knowing that from the Lord you will receive the reward of the inheritance; for you serve the Lord Christ.
>
> —COLOSSIANS 3:23-24

God notices, observes and is motivated by the intention and motivation of your heart. God sees the things you do as an expression of what you keep in your heart. He sees how we serve in our homes, families, churches, ministries, our businesses, and our jobs.

What you do and how you do it is for God a reflection of the way we honor Him; the commitment and the level of priority in which we seek to do what we do well, from the heart, treating it with respect. Internal motivation is reflected in how you do things. And God is worthy that you give Him the best, and that you seek to improve yourself to give Him even more and with greater excellence.

EXCELLENCE HAS A PLAN

Do not lay up for yourselves treasures on earth, where moth and rust destroy and where thieves break in and steal; but lay up for yourselves treasures in heaven, where neither moth nor rust destroys and where thieves do not break in and steal. For where your treasure is, there your heart will be also.

—MATTHEW 6:19-21

Our motivation must always be Jesus, His Word and His will. We do it on earth, but with a heart that loves Him, honors Him and is aware that He is with us.

Then the LORD God took [a]the man and put him in the garden of Eden to [b]tend and keep it. And the LORD God commanded the man, saying, "Of every tree of the garden you may freely eat.

—GENESIS 2:15-16

Before the fall of man, God had established productivity, work and service. The land was blessed and the work was designed for the benefit and satisfaction of man. God designed man and the earth to produce together, to multiply together, and to create resources, livelihoods, and art together.

And the LORD God formed man *of* the dust of the ground, and breathed into his nostrils the breath of life; and man became a living being. The LORD God planted a garden eastward in Eden, and there He put the man whom He had formed. And out of the ground the LORD God made every tree grow that is pleasant to the sight and good for food. The tree of life *was* also in the midst of the garden, and the tree of the knowledge of good and evil. Now a river went out of Eden to water the garden, and from there it parted and became four riverheads. The name of the first *is* Pishon; it *is* the one which skirts the whole land of Havilah, where *there is* gold. And the gold of that land *is* good. Bdellium and the onyx stone *are* there. The name of the second river *is* Gihon; it *is* the one which goes around the whole land of Cush. The name of the third river *is* Hiddekel;[a] it *is* the one which goes toward the east of [b]Assyria. The fourth river *is* the Euphrates. Then the LORD God took [c]the man and put him in the garden of Eden to [d]tend and keep it.

—GENESIS 2:7-15

Note that there was a plan and an order. There was gratification, pleasure and delight. "Adam" in Hebrew means "mankind". "Adamah" in Hebrew means "earth" and is the feminine expression of the word "Adam". In Genesis 3:17 we see that God curses the earth because of the sin of Adam and Eve.

Christ, the second Adam, came to redeem and renew our productive creation and restore gratification and meaning to our ability to produce. Christ came to bless the earth and to establish in us a greater vision, a greater attitude. Christ came to establish the spirit of excellence.

....

Pray for God to give you the anointing of excellence. Wish for it and strive to give your best.

....

YOUR PRESENCE

Christ came to make us a temple of the Holy Spirit. That means you and your God united, together, dreaming, producing, multiplying and taking care of what God adds. Your work is important, your talents are important, your dreams are important. God called many as they worked: Peter, John, James, Matthew, David, Moses, Elijah, and Paul.

In the Garden of Eden, the perfect combination was: family, home, marriage, intimate relationship with God, church, work, productivity. God is passionate about creating and producing. Invite Him into your life, invite Him into your home and your work. Give Him His place and you will see how His blessing will be.

Your presence in us establishes excellence. The in-filling and flowing of the Holy Spirit are a manifestation of excellence.

> "See, I have called by name Bezalel the son of Uri, the son of Hur, of the tribe of Judah. And I have filled him with the Spirit of God, in wisdom, in understanding, in knowledge, and in all *manner of* workmanship, to design artistic works, to work in gold, in silver, in bronze, in cutting jewels for setting, in carving wood, and to work in all *manner of* workmanship. "And I, indeed I, have appointed with him Aholiab the son of Ahisamach, of the tribe of Dan; and I have put wisdom in the hearts of all the gifted artisans, that they may make all that I have commanded you: the tabernacle of meeting, the ark of the Testimony and the mercy seat that *is* on it, and all the furniture of the tabernacle— .
>
> —EXODUS 31: 2-7

This is the first time in the Bible that a person filled with the Holy Spirit is mentioned. Note that it speaks of wisdom, work and creativity, service to God; it speaks of producing something. The Holy Spirit is God of wisdom, intelligence and science in all artwork. God himself sent him. He gave the fullness of his Spirit, the resources, the dream and the vision.

His presence in your life has a creative plan. If we give Him the best of ourselves, that is honor. The opposite is conformism or mediocrity or laziness. That causes your presence and your plan to be restricted or stop flowing.

A great Biblical example of productivity, excellence and work is Solomon. He had authority and power to rule wisely; the power to judge or make decisions wisely; and the power to produce wisely or to bring profit to Israel wisely.

God called him, chose him and anointed him. He gave his best to God; his attitude was excellent.

> So I perceived that nothing *is* better than that a man should rejoice in his own works, for that *is* his [a]heritage. For who can bring him to see what will happen after him?
>
> —ECCLESIASTES 3:22

To work is to serve someone's need. We have to understand that God gives us opportunities to serve and that serving is a good thing that gives meaning and purpose to our lives. To serve is to love God, and God will give us all opportunities to serve, to work.

EXCELLENCE INCLUDES DILIGENCE

Our spirit has to learn the power of diligence. Diligence is related to passion for God.

The plans of the diligent *lead* surely to plenty, but *those of* everyone *who is* hasty, surely to poverty.

—PROVERBS 21:5

Diligence is part of the nature of excellence that God blesses. Plan your dream or your work, and work the plan. You must prepare; learn the plan well, believe in it and act on the plan. Do not put it aside and do not wait later to carry it out. Diligence speaks of now, of executing immediately. Always be active and make every day a day of productivity.

Seek God, His advice, and pray and intercede to God for the plan and for its good results. With God ahead, activate yourself to execute. Put in motion and activate in that opportunity that God has given you.

In all labor there is profit, but idle chatter *leads* only to poverty.

—PROVERBS 14:23

Lack of diligence describes the empty words of impoverishing lips. Diligence is work that persists and is activated without waiting. God is a God who makes himself present to give you wisdom, intelligence and vision. You respond to His presence and the opportunities He gives you with diligence.

Do you see a man *who* [a] excels in his work? He will stand before kings; He will not stand before [b] unknown *men.*

—PROVERBS 22:29

The power of diligence is honor, recognition, influence, good standing, and an anointing to transform cities, nations, and communities. Before kings, He speaks of credibility, influence and giving advice to those in authority.

> Through wisdom a house is built, and by understanding it is established; By knowledge the rooms are filled With all precious and pleasant riches. A wise man *is* strong, Yes, a man of knowledge increases strength; For by wise counsel you will wage your own war, And in a multitude of counselors *there is* safety.
>
> —PROVERBS 24:3-6

This scripture is powerful because it speaks to what God wants to do with you. May our attitude be filled with excellence and diligence to serve, seek change and achieve goals!

Let us be diligent and passionate people. Passion is power because the power of God responds to the passion of man. Jesus was and still is diligent and passionate. He came to seek and save the lost, and continues to do so. Jesus traveled long distances, confronted every obstacle, left eternity, left his glory, paid a price, but He conquered and there is a reward of eternal life for not losing you, for giving us a new opportunity. He never quit. His passion and diligence were intense and never ceased to be so. That is an attitude of powerful excellence!

BALANCE

Order is essential and excellence always establishes God's order. The lack of order cancels the excellence that God blesses. We have to establish balance in all areas of our lives, establishing God's order.

How do we put God first? Reading His word; with a life of prayer; congregating in the church that He has for us; obeying Him, which is the key to success; connecting to the right people and their authorities; resting.

How do we serve the family? Marriage needs quality time. Let us keep the Sabbath day holy; the " Sabbath " is a day of rest, of not working, of sharing with the wife and children. Let's go on vacation with the family and alone as a couple. Let's keep a fair schedule; do not steal the time that corresponds to your family.

TEAM AND DELEGATION

God is a God of teams. If you have a calling and you are married, you cannot do it alone. You need your wife or vice versa. Both are needed, because God is a team God. God gave Moses a structure of order to shepherd the people. We are all necessary for God to appease His people.

We have people, ministers, pastors under pastoral care who guide, disciple and minister to the people who seek God's advice. As long as there is order and they are under pastoral care, there is no problem. This is called the Ministry of Biblical Guidance and Ministry.

For by wise counsel you will wage your own war, And in a multitude of counselors *there is* safety.

—PROVERBS 24:6

∙∙

Victory talks about avoiding failure;
achieve goals, power to win in the
midst of war. It is to fully enjoy.

∙∙

Better a handful *with* quietness Than both hands full, *together with* toil and grasping for the wind. Then I returned, and I saw vanity under the sun: There is one alone, without [a]companion: He has neither son nor brother. Yet *there is* no end to all his labors, Nor is his eye satisfied with riches. *But he never asks,* "For whom do I toil and deprive myself of good?" This also *is* vanity and a [b]grave misfortune. Two *are* better than one, Because they have a good reward for their labor. For if they fall, one will lift up his companion. But woe to him *who is* alone when he falls, For *he has* no one to help him up. Again, if two lie down together, they will keep warm; But how can one be warm *alone?*

—ECCLESIASTES 4:6-11

We can't do it alone; we need a team. God's order is God first; the family; and work and ministry. In the fear of God, we establish his order, because when we respect and honor him, we also honor His Word. We cannot disconnect from honoring Him always.

Chapter 7

OBEDIENCE BLESSES

"Then it shall come to pass, because you listen to these judgments, and keep and do them, that the Lord your God will keep with you the covenant and the mercy which He swore to your fathers.

—Deuteronomy 7:12

Obedience is a learned attitude. The Word says that He gives us the strength to get riches in order to fulfill the covenant, the same one that He confirmed to your ancestors by means of an oath. He made a covenant with a man named Abraham. The Bible calls Abraham the Father of Faith. Abraham operated in grace, before the cross. He did not operate in the law. This man believed God and the Bible says that his faith justified him. We are justified by faith in the Son of God.

This is the covenant that God made with Abraham. God told him:

- I am going to bless you.
- I will give you lands flowing with milk and honey.
- Your enemies will be my enemies.
- Whoever blesses you, I bless him.
- Whoever curses you, I curse him.
- I will give you all the land that the soles of your feet walk on.
- I will multiply your seed.
- When your children and your children's children sow, I will bless that sowing and I will multiply it a hundred times one.

God made a covenant with Abraham because there was a purpose, a vision. Abraham responded to God saying: Amen, I believe it. That was enough for the Lord to seal that covenant. Everything has to do with the redemption of the human being.

Just as Abraham believed God, and it was accounted to him for righteousness. Therefore know that *only* those who are of faith are sons of Abraham. And the Scripture, foreseeing that God would justify the Gentiles by faith, preached the gospel to Abraham beforehand, *saying,* "In you all the nations shall be blessed. So then those who *are* of faith are blessed with believing Abraham".

—GALATIANS 3:6-9

So, the true children of Abraham are those who put their faith in God. We are children of God by faith in His son Jesus Christ. We are children of Abraham by faith in God, and hence God announced that through Abraham all nations would be blessed. All who put their faith in Christ participate in the same blessing that Abraham received because of his faith. And through Christ Jesus, God blessed the gentiles with the same blessing that He promised Abraham, so that believers might receive, through faith, the promised Holy Spirit (see Galatians 3:14). Now the blessing would not be only for the Hebrew people, but in Christ Jesus for the Gentiles as well.

In the covenant that God made with Abraham we can see the following:

1. Earth to form a nation (Earth)
2. Resources to finance a nation (blessing)
3. His divine support, His divine protection and His blessing, as long as the covenant is maintained (perpetuity).

We can read in Genesis 26:12-14, how God followed and continues to fulfill His covenant to this day, multiplying what was promised to his generations. It is important to note that Isaac received the continuity of the covenant that Abraham had made with God. When Isaac planted his crops that year, he reaped a hundred times more grain than he had planted, because the Lord blessed him.

Genesis 22:1-12 says that God tested Abraham's faith. Isaac saw his father's example of obedience to God, when he asked him to use him as a sacrificial lamb. Both obeyed trusting in God, one in offering him as a sacrificial lamb and the other trusting in his father and in God. With this obedience of Isaac in believing them both, he validated God's covenant with his father, Abraham.

Abraham's obedience was an ultimate and supernatural obedience. Note that it was a test. Abraham needed to develop absolute trust in God. [PO] The purpose of trials is that we can exercise our faith. [/PO] He obeyed, God rescued him and affirmed him. Abraham lived the rest of his life with a one hundred percent convinced heart.

> For thus says the High and Lofty One Who inhabits eternity, whose name *is* Holy:
> "I dwell in the high and holy *place,* With him *who* has a contrite and humble spirit,
> To revive the spirit of the humble, And to revive the heart of the contrite ones.
> —ISAIAH 57:15

Obedience brings humility and provides the capacity for perseverance. Humility is the fruit of obedience and fear of God. It is a balance; not believe yourself superior, nor inferior. You must be prudent and considerate to eliminate pride or a sense of superiority in your life.

Let's see in the Bible many examples of disobedience and obedience to God, and its eternal consequences. In 1 Samuel 15:22, referring to the case of King Saul, it says that "to obey is better than sacrifice, *And* to heed than the fat of rams".

....

Obedience brings humility and provides the capacity for perseverance.

....

Disobedience led King Saul to sin and it cost him God's call on his life. Obedience to His Word, obedience to what He puts in your heart, is the fruit of your intimacy with Him.

God's blessing is always in accordance with man's obedience. It is His will to bless you. Your obedience is the way to receive that blessing. Another example of obedience and disobedience is Solomon, to whom God gave the following:

1. Excellence in governing wisely (authority)
2. Excellence in judging wisely (settings and administration)
3. Excellence in producing wealth (producing profits, companies)

But one day, due to the influence of the wrong woman, he disconnected from the commandments and the voice of God. There was no more obedience... and everything collapsed.

Let's take a look at the history:

For it was so, when Solomon was old, that his wives turned his heart after other gods; and his heart was not [a]loyal to the LORD his God, as *was* the heart of his father David. For Solomon went after Ashtoreth the goddess of the Sidonians, and after Milcom[b] the abomination of the Ammonites. Solomon did evil in the sight of the LORD, and did not fully follow the LORD, as *did* his father David. Then Solomon built a [c]high place for Chemosh the abomination of Moab, on the hill that *is* east of Jerusalem, and for Molech the abomination of the people of Ammon. And he did likewise for all his foreign wives, who burned incense and sacrificed to their gods. So the LORD became angry with Solomon, because his heart had turned from the LORD God of Israel, who had appeared to him twice, and had commanded him concerning this thing, that he should not go after other gods; but he did not keep what the LORD had commanded. Therefore the LORD said to Solomon, "Because you have done this, and have not kept My covenant and My statutes, which I have commanded you, I will surely tear the kingdom away from you and give it to your servant. Nevertheless I will not do it in your days, for the sake of your father David; I will tear it out of the hand of your son. However I will not tear away the whole kingdom; I will give one tribe to your son for the sake of My servant David, and for the sake of Jerusalem which I have chosen.

—1 KINGS 11:4-13

Beware of wrong relationships; they can lead you to disobedience. Solomon was seduced, and that led him to honor other gods.

....

Obedience to His Word is the expression of love that God seeks.

....

Chapter 8

OBEDIENCE: PRELUDE TO MULTIPLICATION

But if you look carefully into the perfect law that sets you free, and if you do what it says and don't forget what you heard, then God will bless you for doing it.

—JAMES 1:25 NLT

God has designed a plan for each of His children in this world. Every entrepreneur has been gifted with talents and skills for business and it is necessary to be diligent with what we have been given. But above all things, it is essential to be obedient. Consider what is defined as obedience.

THE SIGN THAT GOD SEEKS

God wants to bless us in everything we undertake. Obedience unleashes the blessings found in the book of Deuteronomy, chapter 28:1:14.

Now it shall come to pass, if you diligently obey the voice of the LORD your God, to observe carefully all His commandments which I command you today, that the LORD your God will set you high above all nations of the earth. And all these blessings shall come upon you and overtake you, because you obey the voice of the LORD your God:

"Blessed *shall* you *be* in the city, and blessed *shall* you *be* in the country.

"Blessed *shall be* the [a]fruit of your body, the produce of your ground and the increase of your herds, the increase of your cattle and the offspring of your flocks.

"Blessed *shall be* your basket and your kneading bowl.

"Blessed *shall* you *be* when you come in, and blessed *shall* you *be* when you go out.

"The Lord will cause your enemies who rise against you to be defeated before your face; they shall come out against you one way and flee before you seven ways.

"The Lord will command the blessing on you in your storehouses and in all to which you set your hand, and He will bless you in the land which the Lord your God is giving you.

"The Lord will establish you as a holy people to Himself, just as He has sworn to you, if you keep the commandments of the Lord your God and walk in His ways. Then all peoples of the earth shall see that you are called by the name of the Lord, and they shall be afraid of you. And the Lord will grant you plenty of goods, in the fruit of your body, in the increase of your livestock, and in the produce of your ground, in the land of which the Lord [b]swore to your fathers to give you. The Lord will open to you His good [c]treasure, the heavens, to give the rain to your land in its season, and to bless all the work of your hand. You shall lend to many nations, but you shall not borrow. And the Lord will make you the head and not the tail; you shall be above only, and not be beneath, if you [d]heed the commandments of the Lord your God, which I command you today, and are careful to observe *them*. So you shall not turn aside from any of the words which I command you this day, *to* the right or the left, to go after other gods to serve them.

OBEDIENCE IS THE SIGN THAT WE ARE UNDER COVENANT

Fools, because of their transgression, And because of their iniquities, were afflicted.

—PSALMS 107:1

IS THE SIGN OF A TRUE RELATIONSHIP WITH GOD

Now by this we know that we know Him, if we keep His commandments. He who says, "I know Him," and does not keep His commandments, is a liar, and the truth is not in him. But whoever keeps His word, truly the love of God [a]is perfected in him. By this we know that we are in Him. He who says he abides in Him ought himself also to walk just as He walked.

—1 JOHN 2:3-6

IS ALSO THE SIGN THAT THERE IS OIL IN OUR LAMPS

The Bible makes mention of oil, its purpose and its importance. The oil represents holiness and the anointing of the Holy Spirit. It is that anointing that enables us to break down obstacles, conquer territory, and influence other people through our works on earth.

When we do our part, God does His part. This is how obedience works. Put all His commandments into practice because they are principles that will guide your decisions, your attitudes, your actions under the influence of Biblical principles. Practice constantly hearing the voice of God because we were created to hear the voice of God. He drives you and His voice grows in your heart.

The moment we invite God into our lives, that part of hearing the voice comes to life within us and activates. We have the right to enter the holy of holies. You can hear it through the Bible, the Holy Spirit. The Lord cares about the city where you live, but you are part of that change, with the fruit of your work and your prosperity. A servant has to hear the voice of his Lord and obey it. Obedience is the prelude to multiplication.

OBEDIENCE TO EARTHLY AUTHORITIES

As businessmen we need to be fair and upright in everything. In every city and in every country, there are regulations for businesses and companies. Avoiding them is going against the law. Not respecting the laws imposed by the authorities make us fall into a serious fault. With the exception of the case that those laws go against the laws and principles of God, we, as businessmen, must conform to the laws and regulations established by the earthly authorities.

In the case of the family, the woman, even if she is an entrepreneur, must submit to her husband. We must also honor our mentors, be humble. David went from being a shepherd of sheep, to an assignment from his father and then to God's assignment, to later becoming king of the nation of Israel. His obedience was rewarded by God at every step.

··

God uses human authorities to launch you into the prophetic greatness of God that He has for you.

··

THE CALL TO ENTREPRENEURS

There is an anointing of the Spirit of God on Latin American businessmen. It is a powerful pioneer anointing. You will do what other people or families have never done: you will do new things; you will conquer new territories. The power to do all this demands a humble heart, a heart to set yourself apart for Him, a heart to honor Him; be faithful to your partner, not go for the money. It is an exaggerated anointing that you must see as a call, as a divine assignment; not like a job.

In the Bible we see how the Lord, over and over again, called entrepreneurs, and how He gave many of them the ability to multiply. Abraham, the first man who believed Him, the Father of Faith, was a businessman whose cattle multiplied. He used Peter, the first to preach under the anointing of the Holy Spirit, to start his church and grow it, and he was another entrepreneur. When the apostle Paul arrived in Europe, the first person who attended him was the first businesswoman, Lidia, also the first person who accepted Christ as her savior.

Why? Because it is through entrepreneurs that the Lord can move the world and reach more people in the Great Commission. They are the prosperous people obedient to Him who reach high levels of influence, who are received before nations and governments and manage to execute plans of His Kingdom on earth.

The entrepreneurial anointing is a powerful anointing to place yourself as an influence; so that the heart of God spills out helping, blessing and prospering. What God is going to put in your hands does not compare to anything. What is in your hands is for Him to use as He wants.

The main purpose of the entrepreneurial anointing is to change nations. This anointing applies to businesses, families, ministries, and government. Every person was created by God. Every person is a miracle and every person has a divine purpose and this purpose is multifaceted. There are different areas where you have a share assigned by God. God's true purpose in your life is a set of purposes that together will produce something divine. There are people who, until they fulfill their business mandate, will not fulfill the purpose for which they have been created by God.

POWERFUL INFLUENCE

You read before that the Church that has no influence, has no power. Influence is the foundation for true power to exist. Influence has power over people, industries, nations, and an entire generation. The name of Jesus is the greatest influence, because in the spiritual world everything changes when Jesus is honored. In the name of Jesus all power falls, evil is confused and Satan's agenda is paralyzed.

Jesus is the greatest influence in heaven, and on earth. That influence that He gave us is used to advance, preach and establish dominion; so that the Gospel of Jesus Christ advances, so that every creature can hear the message of God that saves, restores and prospers lives and families. It is used to establish honesty, ethics, cultures and lifestyles that God wants to establish in us, that bless us and protect us from the traps of Satan. There is a war between good and evil. His servants are essential for evil to lose.

> A feast is made for laughter, And wine makes merry;
> But money answers everything.
> —ECCLESIASTES 10:19

> For wisdom is [a]a defense as money is a defense, But the [b]excellence of knowledge is that wisdom gives life to those who have it.
> —ECCLESIASTES 7:12

Money serves evil. Money serves good. Riches serve to advance the Kingdom, eliminate poverty, add value to the community, and preserve future generations. Work is essential for ideas to produce. We are all called to produce, for ourselves and for others.

In prisons, statistics teach us that 90% of prisoners come from poor homes and without a father present.

....

The number one antidote to crime is
called a present dad who provides.

....

In conclusion, the entrepreneurial spirit has divine purposes that influence to transform, protect and multiply the riches for the expansion of the Kingdom, and provide human and Church needs.

You entrepreneurs are the influence that transforms nations.

Chapter 9

THE TITHING AGREEMENT

Bring all the tithes into the storehouse, That there may be food in My house, And try Me now in this, Says the LORD of hosts, "If I will not open for you the windows of heaven And pour out for you such blessing That there will not be room enough to receive it.

—MALACHI 3:10

God's Word exhorts us in this passage from Malachi to be faithful with ten percent of our income. God does not need us to give to Him, but He does need us to be obedient because that is part of our spiritual formation, of strengthening our faith. For that reason, He promises to pour blessing on us until it overflows. He also makes it clear to us that it is an act of disobedience to take a part of what does not belong to us.

> "For I *am* the LORD, I do not change; Therefore you are not consumed, O sons of Jacob.
> Yet from the days of your fathers You have gone away from My ordinances And have not kept *them.* Return to Me, and I will return to you," Says the LORD of hosts. "But you said, 'In what way shall we return?' Do Not Rob God "Will a man rob God? Yet you have robbed Me! But you say, 'In what way have we robbed You?' In tithes and offerings.
> You are cursed with a curse, For you have robbed Me, *Even* this whole nation. Bring all the tithes into the storehouse, That there may be food in My house, And try Me now in this," Says the LORD of hosts, "If I will not open for you the windows of heaven And pour out for you *such* blessing That *there will* not *be room* enough *to receive it.* "And I will rebuke the devourer for your sakes, So that he will not destroy the fruit of your ground, Nor shall the vine fail to bear fruit for you in the field," Says the LORD of hosts; "And

all nations will call you blessed, For you will be a delightful land," Says the LORD of hosts.

—MALACHI 3:6-12

Giving the tithe is an act that represents many things:

- Tithing represents a diligent heart that cares to put God first.
- It shows a heart that decides to honor God in His Word and that embraces His promises.
- The tithe represents that we honor God first and that we believe in what He promised when we tithe.
- Establish the loss of territory of the god Mammon, or devourer, in your life.
- The tithe is the sign that we are in covenant with God so that His power and favor be with us in our work or in our business.
- When you stop tithing, you lose a lot, because there is a favor of God in finances that is conditional on the one who tithes.
- The amount doesn't matter, what matters is the percentage. God asks for ten percent of what is received.
- It's a covenant, an agreement where you do this and God does His part.

God's blessing always has to do with His covenant. In every agreement there are conditions and instructions. The tithe has to do with God's covenant. The covenants that God makes with us are to bless us, for our good. That is why the tithe, as a covenant, multiplies, protects and connects us with its open skies.

> Blessed *is* the man Who walks not in the counsel of the [a]ungodly, Nor stands in the path of sinners, Nor sits in the seat of the scornful; But his delight *is* in the law of the LORD, And in His law he [b]meditates day and night. He shall be like a tree
> Planted by the [c]rivers of water, That brings forth its fruit in its season, Whose leaf also shall not wither; And whatever he does shall prosper.
>
> —PSALM 1:1-3

The act of tithing is an act of obedience, and like any act of obedience, it leaves us with blessing results. As a consequence of obeying, God promises us:

1. To open the skies
2. To rebuke the devourer
3. The reputation will be that everyone will call us blessed. That speaks of God's favor that others can see.

GOD'S SYSTEM FOR RECEIVING IS TITHE AND OFFERING

Tithing is essential to depower the spirit of Babylon, which represents the corrupt world, the greedy and controlling man's system, and also represents injustice. There are three enemies that Satan himself sends to businessmen:

1. fear
2. corruption
3. greed

The tithe is the spiritual principle that destroys the influence of fear, corruption and greed. From lack of money come stress, divorce and the rebellion of the new generations. Why? Because many couples and families do not find the solution to their financial problems because they have not made the decision to tithe. Consequently, the devourer attacks their finances because his goal is to destroy the family. God gives us this pact: if we tithe, He protects our finances from the clutches of the evil one who wants to destroy us. It is a matter of faith and obedience.

Giving God ten percent of our first fruits, of the first thing we receive, we find His support, His power and it is the way the Bible speaks of God's abundance. The Bible specifically says that He will open the windows of heaven. Ten percent is an investment that pays big dividends. It is God's agreement with us that the Bible teaches us how to prosper. It is an agreement, a covenant with great blessings.

Command those who are rich in this present age not to be haughty, nor to trust in uncertain riches but in the living God, who gives us richly all things to enjoy.
—1 TIMOTHY 6:17

In this passage from the New Testament, we see how the importance of knowing how to let go of riches is re-affirmed, not putting our trust in them. For a rich man, or someone who produces a lot, tithing means a large amount of money. But if this person puts his trust in God and obeys with ten percent of his firstfruits, he is demonstrating that his love for God and His Word is greater than his love for riches. On the other hand, for a person who lives from month to month, setting aside ten percent in his budget is an act of obedience and faith, which also produces wonderful results. A person who tithes before knowing if the money is going to reach him is a person who walks by faith and not by sight, a person whose faith in God goes beyond the circumstances. That person will not lack anything, because God is faithful in what He promises.

We can also read in Haggai 2:8-9 about the prosperity that God gives us, as a gift, and tells us clearly to whom all the riches belong:

The silver *is* Mine, and the gold *is* Mine,' says the LORD of hosts. 9 'The glory of this latter [a]temple shall be greater than the former,' says the LORD of hosts. 'And in this place I will give peace,' says the LORD of hosts.

- Everything belongs to our God. Nothing belongs to man. Man can have it today and not have it tomorrow. The man is only the temporary administrator.
- God always has everything.

- God is a generous God. His intention has always been wholeness. God is very interested in your well-being. Your future in Him is a good future.

It is a good thing to receive riches from God and the good health to enjoy them. Enjoying work and accepting what life brings are true gifts from God.

Chapter 10

GOD'S ADVICE

Blessed is the man Who walks not in the counsel of the [a]ungodly, Nor stands in the path of sinners, Nor sits in the seat of the scornful; But his delight is in the law of the LORD, And in His law he [b]meditates day and night. He shall be like a tree Planted by the [c]rivers of water, That brings forth its fruit in its season, Whose leaf also shall not wither; And whatever he does shall prosper.

—PSALMS 1:1-3

The passage begins with the word "blessed"; speaks of supernatural blessing. Talks about things that money can't buy, but God gives them to you. God is with you always, He fights alongside you. It does much more than satisfy you; He gives you abundantly. God continues the teaching of learning to choose and listen to the right people, even to separate the wrong people from us. We must teach our children so that they too learn to separate the right friendships and say goodbye to the wrong people with love.

The Bible is not an ancient book, it is not a man-made book. It is a holy and powerful scripture. The Bible is the Word of God, and God and his Word are one. The God who created heaven and earth is one with the Bible. It is the heart of God, it is the most intimate of God. To deny the Bible is to deny God. Blessed is he who delights and meditates on the law of the Lord. In the Bible there is joy, hope, new beginnings for you. It is a delight to know God through Scripture.

The Bible says that you will be like a tree planted by streams of water because it leads you to a better life. The advice of God takes you to good places, where the streams are. Every drought goes where God's advice is. The Word of God says that everything we do meditating previously on his Word will prosper and we will bear fruit in due time. You will always be in streams of living water and you will not dry up. Whatever you do, God will prosper.

That is the importance of the counsel of God. God's advice is in Holy Scripture and it gives us the correct orientation for all times: to have a great company, to deal with your children, to set up a ministry, for your marriage. In the Bible is God's advice to do everything. The Bible is not just a piece of advice, it has life. It is not to be read simply, but to speak with it.

The power of the Word ministers. When that power is coupled with the anointing of the Holy Spirit and there is an open heart, anything can happen. The Bible, under the anointing power of the Holy Spirit, transforms. I have been transformed by the power of God through the Holy Word of God. The power, without the Word, is not of God. For it to be the power of God, there must be the Word of God. We all need the counsel of God contained in the Word; ignoring it is a form of rebellion and makes us vulnerable.

> Where *there is* no counsel, the people fall; But in the multitude of counselors *there is* safety.
> —PROVERBS 11:14

We need God's advice not to fall. Without the counsel of God we can all fall. Without the advice of God, companies, governments, churches, everything falls. Where there is no wise direction, the people fall. But in the multitude of counselors there is safety. The Word says *"in the multitude of counselors"*, not governors or human specialists who want to control you. But to advise you with the advice of God.

The advice must be in the light of the Bible, not that of men. He has said that everything I do will prosper and

God uses people to advise and speak everything through his Church. He is the God who gives us wise direction and guides us through His Word.

> Without counsel, plans go awry, but in the multitude of counselors they are established.
> —PROVERBS 15:22

God raises men and women as a team with the gift, passion, ability and Biblical revelation to minister and guide our lives with the Word of God.

> Joseph of Arimathea, a prominent council member, who was himself waiting for the kingdom of God, coming and taking courage, went in to Pilate and asked for the body of Jesus.
> —MARK 15:43

Joseph of Arimathea was an entrepreneur, a businessman who had a lot of influence. The Bible says that he was a noble member of the council. "Noble" refers to the fact that he was a respected advisor; someone who earned the respect of people, with a testimony that reflected what he advised. He was a man of the Kingdom of God, fearing God. He was that someone you can go to and find direction, find inspiration. Joseph was a member of a council, of a team where there was wisdom to counsel and help with wise advice. He was a man of personal testimony, who had God's order in his life.

God is a father and as a father He advises us. If you have a father in life, thank God, whether he is a Christian or not. You have to honor and bless him, love him, and, above all, listen to him. Our God is a father. He is a father who is God, and one of his names is counselor. It is one of His personal attributes. He is a father who instructs, guides and advises. He is a father who wants to continue doing so, and He does so through His Church.

It strikes me how God gave the body of His son to Joseph of Arimathea, but first He gave it to a woman. Jesus was subject to the will of God the Father from birth until He died. After He was resurrected, He continued to submit to the will of His father, and God chose a woman for His son to incarnate. God gave the body of His son to a woman, who formed Him in her womb, gave birth to Him, nursed Him, cared for Him, loved Him, touched Him until He became a man. But when He died, that body was under the authority of Pilate and He decided to give it to Joseph, who was a noble businessman, a member of the council. Everything that happened was prophetic. Joseph, with his team, prepared it, placed it in his tomb and there the body was resurrected. The body is the Church of Jesus Christ.

> This also comes from the LORD of hosts, *Who* is wonderful in counsel *and* excellent in [a]guidance.
> —ISAIAH 28:29

In ministry and biblical guidance is where wisdom will grow in your life. The human being, without the advice of God, falls short. When God advises you, you draw closer to Him. As you open your heart to be teachable. and seek guidance, biblical ministry, better and greater relationship you will have with your heavenly Father. He is the God who makes you, your children and your grandchildren grow, because His advice increases wisdom. His ministration frees you from all religion, from all ignorance. His biblical ministry breaks all chains. He is the God who makes you grow, He is the God who heals you, protects you, forms your character for good, confirms you, assures you and transforms you.

> So when they had eaten breakfast, Jesus said to Simon Peter, "Simon, *son* of [a]Jonah, do you love Me more than these?" He said to Him, "Yes, Lord; You know that I [b]love You." He said to him, "Feed My lambs." He said to him again a second time, "Simon, *son* of [c] Jonah, do you love Me?" He said to Him, "Yes, Lord; You know that I [d]love You." He said to him, "Tend My sheep." He said to him the third time, "Simon, *son* of [e]Jonah, do you [f]love Me?" Peter was grieved because He said to him the third time, "Do you love Me?" And he said to Him, "Lord, You know all things; You know that I love You." Jesus said to him, "Feed My sheep.
> —JOHN 21: 15-17).

Peter denied it three times out of fear. On the night the Lord was arrested, Peter cut off a soldier's ear. The Lord took the ear, put it back on the soldier, and healed him. That same night, Peter showed courage, only to fall into cowardice and later deny Christ. All in the same day.

Sometimes we are like Peter. Peter felt bad, he was ashamed and abandoned everything. He felt unworthy to serve the Lord and went back to his business. He had fishing boats and he sold the fish, he was a merchant. The Lord, after He was resurrected, appeared to Peter on the beach, where he had gone to fish and had not caught anything. But at the moment that the Lord walked along that beach, God spoke with Peter, advised him and told him: "Go again". He gave him instructions on what to do to fish.

Peter followed the instructions and caught many fish. But after that he realized that it was Jesus who had spoken to him. Then he abandoned all those fish, that prosperity that he had achieved, jumped into the water and ran towards the Lord. And the Lord prepared a meal for him and they ate.

The Lord is the God who restores; there is nothing in your past that He cannot heal. There is no human error that God does not forgive and whose effects He does not restore. There is nothing that God cannot restore. We have to be like Him: do not judge, do not condemn, do not point. We have to be restorers, walk in grace, in mercy, be that Church that offers new opportunities. God in a glorified body left his greatness and placed himself at Peter's height.

In order to restore someone, God does anything and uses anyone, in the way He wants. At the time of restoration, the sovereignty of God is manifested. There is no human judgment, understanding or reasoning to be able to understand God when He is restoring. God in a glorified body began to cook and served Peter.

When he told Peter to "feed my sheep", He indicated his calling. When He spoke of "feed my sheep," He spoke of leading, counseling, herding His sheep, instructing, guiding, and ministering to them. He wanted to tell him: Bring my advice to my people, food, advice that makes them grow, orient them to who I am and what they are. Guide them, minister to them in what I want for them. Peter becomes the pastoral ministerial office.

We have people, ministers, pastors under pastoral care who guide, disciple and minister to the people who seek God's advice. As long as there is order and they are under pastoral care, there is no problem. This is called the Ministry of Biblical Guidance and Ministering.

> For by wise counsel you will wage your own war, And in a multitude of counselors *there is* safety.
>
> —PROVERBS 24:6

Chapter 11

THINGS THAT STOP SUCCESS IN BUSINESS

*Commit your actions to the LORD,
and your plans will succeed.*

—PROVERBS 16:3 NLT

When a business doesn't prosper as well as it should, there are always reasons. The business leader must be aware of why the business is not prospering.

There are many reasons that can cause business stagnation. But beyond all the reasons of strategic order, administrative problems or incorrect marketing, God's blessing can make us prosper in a supernatural way and open our eyes to correct mistakes and prolong our prosperity. We need God's blessing that comes with superior creativity.

When a business is under covenant with God, things work very differently. When we are born again, having recognized Jesus Christ as our Savior, we have a great advantage: We are children of God!

The Bible says wonderful things about us:

> Do you not know that you are the temple of God and *that* the Spirit of God dwells in you?
> —1 CORINTHIANS 3:16

We are a temple of the Spirit of God, we have access to the presence of God, to the revelation of His Word: the Word that cuts, not the Word that entertains. I mean that the "motivational" style word that does not reveal the truths of the full Gospel does not fulfill its function because it carries the intention of man; it is not the pure Gospel.

The word that entertains is useless, because the sky is not part of the show. Heaven is about uprooting, planting, transforming, releasing, saving, healing, and restoring.

WE HAVE ACCESS TO
THE VOICE OF GOD

When we see the intelligence, creativity, and power in creation, it strengthens our faith. We need to hear the voice of God through the Holy Scriptures, through our times of prayer, in order to develop our faith.

> So then faith *comes* by hearing, and hearing by the word of God.
>
> —ROMANS 10:17

This passage from Romans says that our faith comes by hearing, hearing the voice of God. But in turn, hearing that voice comes from reading the Word of God and the revelation found in it. When we know God in a personal way, we realize that there is nothing impossible for Him. I encourage you to believe with all your heart that there is nothing impossible that God cannot do in your business. You can believe that, from the hand of God, your business will multiply and that you will prosper. Do not put limitations on God with what He wants to do with your business. The idea is that you see your business as a divine assignment, so that you can influence your community and change the culture around you to honor God and His Word. You have to realize that the mind and ability of God is much more than what man can possess.

For God to pour out His favor and multiplication, things must be done correctly. **Your business is your**

assignment. Everything that happens in business happens because the leader makes it happen.

If the leader doesn't provoke it, it doesn't happen.

If the leader doesn't implement it, it doesn't appear out of nowhere.

If the leader does not correct it, it will continue to be wrong.

God puts in your mind and in your heart the right strategies, and you put them in the business.

THE PRODUCT, THE SERVICE AND THE WAY OF OPERATING A COMPANY

The other day I went with my son to a restaurant that sells a good product and has a good location. We went for the quality of the food. There we have a good point. Then it is easy to get to the place. Two points in favor. In that establishment, to be served, you have to order first at the counter and then they bring it to your table. But it so happened that there was a line of eight people and seven employees inside, and yet the line did not move. There was no reason for this, as there were seven employees. Looking around, I realized there were dirty tables, no napkins, and no manager to talk to. None of the employees were doing the most important thing they had to do, due to the lack of leadership, of a manager who was in control of everything. So we left, and I came to the conclusion that there was no person in charge in that place to activate the vision of excellence and maintenance of this restaurant.

As a store owner, I immediately focus on those details, fix the problem, intentionally activate excellence in the business, and pass on that culture to the entire team. Maybe the owner wasn't there, maybe the manager wasn't doing his job. They lost two customers and possibly more over the course of the day.

Business is a place to make money. This guarantees its growth and, therefore, its success. If your business isn't making money, you need to consider the way you're running it.

OTHER ISSUES THAT STOP PROSPERITY

You, as a leader, must establish the place of excellence and correct what you must correct. However, there are external factors that can cause stagnation and loss of money. Some of them could be:

- The product is not in demand
- The competition is taking away sales
- The industry is changing and we must keep pace with these changes and innovate.

We must study the demand for our product, the competition and its effect. On the other hand, markets can be changeable. In recent times we have experienced monumental changes, unexpected and difficult to accept. However, we must adapt.

So far we have talked about the natural point of view of how to run the business. But there is the spiritual part, which is the most important.

THE SPIRITUAL CONNOTATION THAT WE HAVE TO TAKE CARE OF

I'll start with this story, which clearly exemplifies what can happen.

Dave Hodgson has a very good parable about a camel and a man. We must take into account that the camel was created to live in the desert and the man was not. This story is called *The Camel's Nose*:

A man rides his camel through the desert. Suddenly a strong sandstorm comes.The man makes a tent and hides inside to avoid the storm. The camel pokes his nose out and says, "Let me get my nose into your tent so I don't breathe in the sand." The man tells him he's fine and falls asleep. In a while he wakes up and sees the camel with its entire head inside the tent. The camel then tells him: "Let me put my head in so the sand doesn't get into my ears." The man agrees and falls asleep. In a while, the entire camel entered the tent. The tent collapsed and the man died, but the camel survived because camels can be in the middle of sandstorms.

The moral is: "Watch out for the camel's nose, because it will eventually knock your tent down."

In the Bible this happened to several people:

David was a man who had the complete backing of God. David's company was a complete nation. But one day, seeing a naked woman and sending for her, he made a big mistake. He gave way to tempting thoughts, used his power, and his lust destroyed his reign.

We can say that the woman exemplifies the nose of the camel. The camel's neck was when he sent for her, and when his tent fell, that was when his lust destroyed him.

Solomon ... the same lust he inherited from his dad destroyed his kingship. The wisest man dropped the store too.

Another different case was Joshua. He was the leader of the people and connected with God to find the answer as to why they were losing the war against the Amorites. God communicated with the leader and told him what was happening, so that he could correct it.

He did not communicate with the employees, only with the leader, who is the one with the power to change, guide and obey what God reveals and commands. At that time the business was to take power from all the surrounding territories and kings, pending to attack the weakness they saw. This was God's revelation to Joshua so that he would correct what was wrong, act and have victory.

> Then Joshua tore his clothes, and fell to the earth on his face before the ark of the LORD until evening, he and the

elders of Israel; and they put dust on their heads.[7] And Joshua said, "Alas, Lord [a]GOD, why have You brought this people over the Jordan at all—to deliver us into the hand of the Amorites, to destroy us? Oh, that we had been content, and dwelt on the other side of the Jordan! O Lord, what shall I say when Israel turns its [b] back before its enemies? For the Canaanites and all the inhabitants of the land will hear *it,* and surround us, and cut off our name from the earth. Then what will You do for Your great name?" So the LORD said to Joshua: "Get up! Why do you lie thus on your face? Israel has sinned, and they have also transgressed My covenant which I commanded them. For they have even taken some of the [c]accursed things, and have both stolen and deceived; and they have also put *it* among their own stuff. Therefore the children of Israel could not stand before their enemies, *but* turned *their* backs before their enemies, because they have become doomed to destruction. Neither will I be with you anymore, unless you destroy the accursed from among you.

—JOSHUA 7:6-12

God told him that his people had sinned. They had made a covenant that they would not take anything. And they were not all, it was a single family; but that action hurt everyone.

This is where most Christian entrepreneurs fail the test. This has nothing to do with the grace of God, but rather with the justice of God. Grace is to save you and to transform you. The ten commandments remain before and after the cross. God commanded them to destroy the anathema, which offended God by breaking the covenant. God called him anathema. God told him not to take anything from the enemy's camp. None of this mattered to them. Those were unjust riches, that God did not want in His people. But Aham paid no attention; Acam means: "the one who accumulates".

> So Joshua rose early in the morning and brought Israel by their tribes, and the tribe of Judah was taken. He brought the clan of Judah, and he took the family of the Zarhites; and he brought the family of the Zarhites man by man, and Zabdi was taken. Then he brought his household man by man, and Achan the son of Carmi, the son of Zabdi, the son of Zerah, of the tribe of Judah, was taken. Now Joshua said to Achan, "My son, I beg you, give glory to the LORD God of Israel, and make confession to Him, and tell me now what you have done; do not hide *it* from me." And Achan answered Joshua and said, "Indeed I have sinned against the LORD God of Israel, and this is what I have done: When I saw among the spoils a beautiful Babylonian garment, two hundred shekels of silver, and a wedge of gold weighing fifty shekels, I [a]coveted them and took them. And there they are, hidden in the earth in the midst of my tent, with the silver under it."
>
> —JOSHUA 7:16-21

Greed is the beginning of the dominion of the god Mammon, since Acam took...

- A Babylonian cloak
- 200 shekels of silver
- 1 gold ingot

Aham had previously coveted it. The anathema was covetousness, disobedience, and putting his security and trust in what he could accumulate, and not in God. The anathema was that Aham did not obey Joshua's authority; is that he had something hidden in the camp. And God didn't want it.

Your trust must be in the provision that God will give you. Our confidence should not be in profit. When the profits come, don't see it as profit, but as God's provision. The moment you put your trust in what you earned, it becomes anathema and God is offended. The important thing is the supply, not the quantity. Earnings should not determine your future. Your future must be in the one that provides everything you need. Aham's heart was filled with idolatry. That led him to have something hidden in his camp, something that God did not want. As a consequence of this action, God stopped His favor on all the people. They returned to the desert and lost their reputation until Joshua took them out and brought out the curse.

BEWARE OF TRAPS

If you are going to involve God in your business, you need to honor Him, obey Him, and carry out His instructions. You must act according to the statutes that He has given us in His Word.

Do not involve God as an amulet to give you profit, that is anathema. God cannot be fooled. You must involve him, first because it is your assignment from Him, then because He is your provider, and you are going to represent Him worthily.

Watch out for that trap. Do not look to God as an amulet for prosperity. Check the intentions of your heart. Prosperity and success will come with your support, when we do the right thing, when we have an authentic heart and do things right. There is a part that is our work, it must be done with intelligence, dedication and justice. The importance of prayer and being exposed to the Word of God is that God shows you where to run your business and what is wrong, what needs to be corrected.

THINGS YOU SHOULD ALWAYS KEEP IN MIND AND NEVER ABANDON AS AN ENTREPRENEUR:

- Prayer
- The Word that cuts like a two-edged sword and sets you free
- Seek God until He shows you why the business is not prospering.
- Be careful what you allow or not in your business. It depends on you that you have God's blessing. God is a God of order. Remember that you are the business.

- Don't stop being generous with those who are in need. God provides for you to bless others.
- Entrepreneurs must be men and women of prayer and consult God about everything. We need to be people in constant search of God, His guidance and His wisdom.

WATCH OUT FOR THE CAMEL'S NOSE!

These are some examples of behaviors that become anathemas, that do not please God and that lead to your business not prospering.

- Arrogance
- Pride
- Lack of forgiveness
- Abuse of power
- Toxic people who are in the business or close to you exerting influence
- God doesn't want you to be a "workaholic" as workaholics are called in English. It is important to Him that you give priority to your family.
- Pornography
- Theft, cheat or lies

In the natural part you are the business. Excellence should be your priority.

In the spiritual part, you must know that God loves you. He is a God of Justice, who expects you to be exposed to the Word of God that cuts like a two-edged sword and sets you free.

Always put your eyes on the provider and not on the provision.

Chapter 12

LET'S BE THE INFLUENCE THE WORLD NEEDS

Let them do good, that they be rich in good works, ready to give, willing to share, storing up for themselves a good foundation for the time to come, that they may lay hold on eternal life.

—1 TIMOTHY 6:18-19

Tell them to use their money to do good. They should be rich in good works and generous to those in need, always being ready to share with others.

—1 TIMOTHY 6:18 NLT

The influence, the power and the favor of the riches made by the power of God are not to hide them, they are not to compromise them; they are for use. With the power that riches give, we must exert influence around us in such a way that we can build a platform where God's integral blessing flows in society.

God uses them to establish His will and His testimony. Doing good speaks of exerting influence in such a way that others receive benefits. When He mentions *"good deeds"* speaks of being active in doing good. When He says we are *"generous"* speaks of giving. The word *"willing"* speaks of being attentive, or worrying.

THE RICHES GIVEN BY GOD SERVE TO:

- Help others
- Dressing the naked
- Finance missions
- Give financial strength to your church
- Buy territories
- Transform nations
- Leave inheritance to our children

One of the causes of poverty is that the previous generation did not leave an inheritance and we are called to leave an inheritance to our children. Jehovah Jireh manifests himself through his sons. We are the ones called to finance God's Vision. God is calling men and women in this generation whom He can entrust with His riches.

Abraham flowed in the power to get riches. Isaac went in search of the power to make riches. To Joseph, God sovereignly entrusted the administration of the riches of Egypt, and thanks to his influence he saved his brothers and his father from starvation.

King David, King Solomon flowed mightily in God's power to get riches. They built a safe and powerful nation while honoring God. Today, we see the nation of Israel flowing greatly in God's power to build wealth. Thanks to their powerful economy, they can survive.

That power is for the church of Jesus Christ too. It was in the flow that His body was buried and it was in that flow that His body was resurrected. Let us always remember that Jesus rose as King and Lord of the Universe.

INFLUENTIAL MEN AND WOMEN IN HISTORY

Joseph of Arimathea

Now when evening had come, there came a rich man from Arimathea, named Joseph, who himself had also become a disciple of Jesus. This man went to Pilate and asked for the body of Jesus. Then Pilate commanded the body to be given to him. When Joseph had taken the body, he wrapped it in a clean linen cloth, and laid it in his new tomb which he had hewn out of the rock; and he rolled a large stone against the door of the tomb, and departed.

—MATTHEW 27:57-60

Joseph of Arimathea was a disciple of Jesus and flowed in the power of God to get rich. His influence was very powerful, stronger than that of the high priest. He had credibility and access to the highest authority in the Roman government, Pilate. He asked for the body of Jesus after he was crucified and they gave him the body.

God the Father placed in his hands the dead body of His son. At that moment, at that specific time, there was nothing more valuable to God than the dead body of Jesus, and God the Father trusted Joseph of Arimathea. Joseph prepared it and placed it in a private tomb that belonged to him. There God the Father resurrected the body of His son Jesus Christ.

The influence of Joseph of Arimathea was not only before man, but also before God. Joseph sought out the priest Nicodemus to help him prepare the body for burial and future resurrection. Together with the women who served Jesus, they prepared the body.

This is a prophetic picture of what God wants to do with Christian businessmen. The body is the Church.

••

The influence of the businessmen united with the priests and the call that God makes to the Christian woman to serve, will bring a powerful revival in the nations.

••

Timothy

Let them do good, that they be rich in good works, ready to give, willing to share, storing up for themselves a good foundation for the time to come, that they may lay hold on eternal life.

—1 TIMOTHY 6:18-19

Timothy was a powerful influence in the government. God will put His disciples to flow in the power to get riches in front of governors, presidents and kings, so that the will of God may be fulfilled on earth. That is why Paul tells Timothy: Teach the rich who come to your church to use their money to do good. Good is God's will on earth.

Lydia of Thyatira

And on the Sabbath day we went out of the city to the riverside, where prayer was customarily made; and we sat down and spoke to the women who met *there.* Now a certain woman named Lydia heard *us.* She was a seller of purple from the city of Thyatira, who worshiped God. The Lord opened her heart to heed the things spoken by Paul. And when she and her household were baptized, she begged *us,* saying, "If you have judged me to be faithful to the Lord, come to my house and stay." So she persuaded us.

—ACTS 16:13-15

Lydia of Thyatira was a businesswoman. She was a merchant of purple cloth and only rich people could buy her product from her. She owned a house. She became a disciple of the Apostle Paul. She is considered the first person in Europe who was born again, who became a Christian. With her purchasing power she financed Paul's ministry and served him with his goods and estates. Because of her influence, many came to hear Paul preach and many were saved.

The first church in Europe, in Philippi, was founded by the Apostle Paul. The first to be baptized in that church was Lydia. Lydia was engaged to Paul and assisted him, she was a church leader and that church started in her house (see Acts 16:40).

We can say that the power to get rich is an undeserved favor. It is His Holy Spirit within you, active to bring about prosperity, inspiring you and making you dream, giving you creative abilities, abilities to adjust to changes and use them to prosper.

HOW CAN WE BE AN INFLUENCE IN THESE TIMES?

When the world sees that we are united helping and blessing the community, they admire us and that is how they evangelize. When the spiritual world sees that our influence is powerful on the thrones, they will respect us and will have to back down.

When we use the influence God gives us to establish His will, the nation prospers, new generations grow up in peace and security, and God's values are honored.

LAST WORDS

What is the secret of influential businessmen, those who are received where they want to be received... those whose opinions are taken into account and included in the most important decisions of society?

The time is today, we are in grace. The secret is a dual and intentional preparation: business principles that have worked for centuries, on the powerful foundation of God's principles. Their favor, their multiplication and our obedience form influential entrepreneurs who even make themselves needed by those whom we want to influence.

To know the secrets in detail and how to turn them into effective action, we have to read the entire book. Here I summarize the inescapable.

1. Let's put God first. Let's not do anything without asking Him.
2. Let's learn the power of obedience... even if we don't understand.
3. Let us practice the attitude and principle of excellence in everything.

4. Let's make tithing an essential part of our lifestyle. It is an agreement or covenant that brings great benefits, and the best investment we can make.
5. Let us be influence with determination under His will.

Responding to God's call to be entrepreneurs for Him and for His plans and purposes requires being aware that, in addition to money and prosperous businesses, we need spiritual power and resources because our assignment represents a high level of spiritual warfare. The movement that I have prophesied and that gave me the need to write this book has already begun stealthily in the United States, Australia and Latin America. I mentioned earlier that Latin American entrepreneurs and women have a specific call from God and a powerful anointing in this move.

There will be a better future and great opportunities, but we must overcome the persecution. If we stop fighting, the Church ends and so does the power that corresponds to us to claim. It is up to us entrepreneurs to win the way the leaders do in all spheres. What do those of us who feel called to this task do?

World leaders pay attention to entrepreneurs. They serve them. Their advice carries weight because it has influence and power. The strategy is:

*   Create and develop good relationships with government authorities, business, education

and other organizations that can bring about changes in God's agenda.

- It must be remembered that the correct authority is the one that gives, not the one that receives. The ultimate purpose of exerting influence is to establish the priority of the Word, which is what opens doors.
- Fulfill God's plan in favor of the future of the next generation, of whom we are spiritual parents. This generation can be fixed if we do our job without fear.
- Inspire those who dream of having companies, not for the love of money itself, but for what an entrepreneur can achieve from an influential position for the kingdom of God.

It is my vision that every businessman of God reaches such a level of influence, that he has access to the most prominent figures of power in governments and nations, and is listened to, taken into account and considered within the decision-making that can produce the changes that God wants for His children and the whole world. I have seen it, I believe it, and I educate and will continue to educate each entrepreneur under my coverage and outside of it to have the influence that leads us to make God's plans and the supreme purpose of the Great Commission a reality.

We must show the world a behavior of obedience, we must be examples of success in what we undertake, having been guided by the hand of God. That is the way we can impact the world. We have a great mission!

> You are the salt of the earth. But what good is salt if it has lost its flavor? Can you make it salty again? It will be thrown out and trampled underfoot as worthless. You are the light of the world—like a city on a hilltop that cannot be hidden. No one lights a lamp and then puts it under a basket. Instead, a lamp is placed on a stand, where it gives light to everyone in the house. In the same way, let your good deeds shine out for all to see, so that everyone will praise your heavenly Father.
>
> —MATTHEW 5:13-16 NLT

ABOUT THE AUTHOR

Pastor Frank López was born in Havana, Cuba. He came to the United States when he was one year old. He became an electrical engineer and business administrator, graduated from the University of Miami. For many years he stood out as a successful businessman, with managerial and administrative experience. At the age of 33, he gave his life to the Lord, and since then, he has shown a deep interest in placing his knowledge at the service of the Christian community, founding entities such as "Amanecer Christian Network", a radio station that broadcast for many years from the city of Miami, and the music label "Rejoice Music".

He is the founder and senior pastor of Iglesia Doral Jesus Worship Center in Miami, one of the fastest growing and most influential congregations in South Florida. His teachings are causing a great impact both locally and in Latin America. His message has been characterized by the restoration of the leadership, the family and the people of God in general.

He hosts the television show "A time of hope", broadcast on several channels in Miami and by Enlace Internacional, as well as its radio version through a Univisión radio station. He is the author of two books: *El Dios que restaura* y *Bendecidos son los discípulos*, published by Casa Creación.

Pastor Frank has a fervent desire to continue working hard so that each believer is restored and achieves the purpose that God has prepared for each person.

He lives in South Florida with his wife, Zayda, and their children, Frankie, Daniel, and Isabella.

✉ pastor@iglesiadoral.org
⊙ franklopezjwc
🅕 franklopezjwc
🌐 www.iglesiajwc.com

THE
SECRETS
OF GOD'S GREAT
ENTREPRENEURS

- Their business vision reflect the larger vision of two.
- They are wise stewards of the goods they receive.
- They are committed to being instruments of God's plans.
- Nothing stops them because their eyes are on Jesus, and not on themselves.
- They have vision to multiply, faith to believe and diligence to work.
- They understand that prayer is the prelude to doing and wanting.
- They consult God about their decisions.
- They put God first.
- They honor the covenant of tithe and offering.
- They cry out to Him for the anointing and the power to make riches.
- They know and profess the power of obedience.

- They know that the instructions for their life, their businesses and their success are in their intimacy with God.
- They seek God's full backing in everything they undertake.
- They know that God will ask great deeds of them, will reward them greatly, and they obey Him.
- They trust; they know there is no such thing as failure in God.
- They build businesses with a generational vision, involving their children.
- They know that the Gospel is the transforming power of God to take the ordinary and make it extraordinary.
- They are sure that with God they will prosper.
- They know God's plan: order, structure, excellence, obedience, and diligence.
- They pray that God will give them the anointing of excellence.
- They believe in God's covenant promises.
- They always put their eyes on the provider and not on the provision.

Jesus Worship Center

1900 NW 89 PL. DORAL
MIAMI-FL. 33172 USA
WWW.IGLESIAJWC.ORG

NOTES

NOTES

NOTES

NOTES

NOTES

NOTES

NOTES

NOTES

NOTES

www.ingramcontent.com/pod-product-compliance
Lightning Source LLC
Chambersburg PA
CBHW050642190326
41458CB00008B/2388